JESUS IN HELL

Four Days

By: Michael P. Green

Gotham Books

30 N Gould St.
Ste. 20820, Sheridan, WY 82801
https://gothambooksinc.com/

Phone: 1 (307) 464-7800

© 2024 *Michael P. Green*. All rights reserved.

No part of this book may be reproduced, stored in a retrieval system, or transmitted by any means without the written permission of the author.

Published by Gotham Books (August 7, 2024)

ISBN: 979-8-3303-5094-0 (P)
ISBN: 979-8-3303-3075-1 (E)

Because of the dynamic nature of the Internet, any web addresses or links contained in this book may have changed since publication and may no longer be valid.

The views expressed in this work are solely those of the author and do not necessarily reflect the views of the publisher, and the publisher hereby disclaims any responsibility for them.

Contents

A Message from the Author: vii
Part I: Bethesda 1
Part II: Death 7
Part III: Hell 21
Part IV: The Gentiles in Hell 53
Part V: The Resurrection 65
Bible Verses: 67

God over all, in all, creator of all; I ask you to help me in the work. I ask this in the name of your son Jesus, the Mediator of the New Covenant in His Blood; I honor you as all powerful, Jehovah God and ask that you justify the expectation that is already performed by your words which were spoken over me from the beginning. Allow your holy spirit to enter into me and keep evil from entering into your rest. I wrote God, he wrote the rest.

John 14:31

But that the world may know that I love the Father; and as the Father gave me commandment, even so I do. Arise, let us go hence.

Job 23:14

For he performeth the thing that is appointed for me: and many such things are with him.

Matthew 5:13-16

Ye are the salt of the earth: but if the salt have lost his savour, wherewith shall it be salted? it is thenceforth good for nothing, but to be cast out, and to be trodden under foot of men. Ye are the light of the world. A city that is set on an hill cannot be hid. Neither do men light a candle, and put it under a bushel, but on a candlestick; and it giveth light unto all that are in the house. Let your light so shine before men, that they may see your good works, and glorify your Father which is in heaven.

Deuteronomy 32:3

Because I will publish the name of the LORD: ascribe ye greatness unto our God.

Psalms 90:16-17

Let thy work appear unto thy servants, and thy glory unto their children. And let the beauty of the LORD our God be upon us: and establish thou the work of our hands upon us; yea, the work of our hands establish thou it.

Hebrews 6:10-11

For God is not unrighteous to forget your work and labour of love, which ye have shewed toward his name, in that ye have ministered to the saints, and do minister. And we desire that every one of you do shew the same diligence to the full assurance of hope unto the end:

1Peter 4:6

For this cause was the gospel preached also to them that are dead, that they might be judged according to men in the flesh, but live according to God in the spirit.

1Corinthians 2:1-2

But I determined this with myself, that I would not come again to you in heaviness.

For if I make you sorry, who is he then that maketh me glad, but the same which is made sorry by me?

A Message from the Author:

I thank God for the opportunity to complete another book. I have many personal traits which should keep me from writing, but God saw fit to provide his grace, which propels me and makes me more than I am. He has made me do greater things than I could alone. I thank you God for what is and ask that this work be a blessing in the lives of your children. I send this letter to the Ebeneezer Baptist Church.

Website: http://michaelgreenauthor.blogspot.com/

Email: michael.green133@gmail.com

Part I: Bethesda

Josiah was raised in Geba, which sits as a township just outside of Jerusalem, in the land of Benjamin. Geba is not one of the best known villages in the surrounds but it has good enough people, trinketry, and livestock to be better known and boast as well as any other village. It is a place of herdsmen and artisans; people familiar with hard work. Josiah's people were descended from the tribe of Naphtali and in fact he lived, until seven years of age, in of all places Chorazin. Both Chorazin and Geba are built onto the side of a hill, that is all the two cities have in common. The Jews of Chorazin were not good Jews; they had abandoned the commandments and took on the ways of the gentiles around them. They worshiped the gods of the gentiles and kept their rituals & superstitions. The people of Chorazin were very superstitious, in fact I note this to their shame; they placed a bust of Medusa's head over the door of the temple to make the unseen seen and stop any evil spirit in its tracks.

They believed in secret mysteries, divination of spirits, and worshiped idols; they even blasphemed the pillars before the temple with their oaths. The people of Chorazin had been assimilated into Roman culture and believed themselves to be citizens of Rome, not of Israel. The Chorazins were farmers, however they did not raise livestock. They used the fertile basaltic soils surrounding the city to grow grains. These sowers were admired for their ability to harvest crops months before others due to this favorable atmosphere for herb growth. Josiah had seen these things as a child, but much of his memories were as limited as he.

He came into the world without the use of his legs; he was a cripple since birth and had lived with the infirmity for some thirty-eight years. Mind you! It is not uncommon for babes born in this state to suffer a pitiable death. Many times Josiah yearned to have suffered this fate, the fate of those that come into the world at an untimely moment. For death is a sly opportunist! Josiah had hoped that his body would reject life as others had, but in most respects his body was strong and well adjusted to his disability. He had large strong hands, beautiful feet, keen eyes, and an abundance of energy. All he really needed was a positive disposition, with that he could not only survive but also thrive.

At the age of seven Josiah and his parents had journeyed from Chorazin to Jerusalem because it was told them that there was a pool near Jerusalem, that healed the infirmed of their brokenness. The family waited at the pool for a time, but had only seen one man healed, not their son. They eventually settled in Geba, determined to acquire this same healing for Josiah. His parents went about their lives as farmers but kept a close vigil on their son as he remained poolside. As time passed Josiah buried both of his parents but still had not attained his desire of being made whole. He waited near the pool with thousands of sick, lame, halt people; all of them waiting on this same healing.

He had found another family as he waited there with the only people in the world that could see him and his condition through his eyes.

His parents loved him, but he surmised that even they could not know the depths of his tormenting struggle. Josiah knew everyone there, even the squatters that arrived daily were quickly indoctrinated with their society's rules and their names and circumstances were made known to the community.

Dondeus, was an ancient man of God who thought it his duty station to wait at the pool for the Messiah. He knew everyone there because he had been poolside longer than anyone else. He was blind but thought it not a disability, in fact he had helped several people into the pool at the time of the troubling of the water. He led them to their healing. Many believed that he could see the angel, but others believed that he was the angel. All other men there were patients waiting to be healed but Dondeus waited on the infirmed as if he were their nurse. When a new person arrived it was he who indoctrinated them into society and told everyone their story. They were instantly accepted because no one could resist a Dondeus introduction. Dondeus worked poolside many years fulfilling the duties of his station all the while awaiting the showing of the Messiah. It was he who helped Josiah from the pool and helped to bury both of his parents when it was their season. No other friend would dare leave their squattery to perform this service. Everyone was saddened when Dondeus died and went to be with his fathers. It was after the death of Dondeus that Josiah began to read the Torah as he waited by the pool. After some months of mourning for beloved Dondeus, life found a new consistency at Bethesda.

On most days the pool was a very quiet orderly place. Each pool had ten lame elders who did not move from their post because they could not move; the heathen jokingly referred to them as Sadducees. The elders were lain poolside and each watched continuously for the same sign.

In truth for most of the year the watchers were not needed because this sign occurred each year before the Feast of the Jews, but after the Festival of Tabernacles. Everyone knows that the Feast of the Jews is held to celebrate passover; it commemorates the sparing of the firstborn sons from the tenth plague in Egypt, just before the Exodus. Tabernacles is a festival that celebrates the abundance from the fields given to man by God. At the end of the year a feast is held to celebrate what has been gathered from labors out of the field.

Tabernacles is the third major feast of the year as required in the Law of Moses. The story of Josiah, The Preacher of Hellfire, begins here.

After this there was a feast held by the Jews; and Jesus went up to Jerusalem to attend. Now there is at Jerusalem by the sheep market a pool, which is called in the Hebrew tongue Bethesda, having five porches. In these lay a great multitude of impotent folk, of blind, halt, withered, dispositions waiting for the water in the pool to begin to move. For an angel went down at a certain season into the pool, and troubled the water: whosoever then first after the troubling of the water stepped in was made whole of whatsoever disease he had.

Josiah knew this because he had laid there at the pool for thirty-eight years and watched many people find healing through the angel of God which troubled the waters. Then one day as he waited at the pool a man walked up to Josiah and looked at him intently as he spoke.

He said, Wilt thou be made whole? The impotent man answered him, Sir, I have no man, when the water is troubled, to put me into the pool: but while I am coming, another steppeth down before me. Jesus saith unto him, Rise, take up thy bed, and walk. And immediately the man was made whole, and took up his bed, and walked: and on the same day was the sabbath. The Jews therefore said unto him that was cured, It is the sabbath day: it is not lawful for thee to carry thy bed. He answered them, He that made me whole, the same said unto me, Take up thy bed, and walk. Then asked they him, What man is that which said unto thee, Take up thy bed, and walk? And he that was healed wist not who it was: for Jesus had conveyed himself away, a multitude being in that place.

Immediately Josiah went to the temple to praise God and offer the appropriate sacrifice for his healing as shown in the law of Moses, but because he had not worked, and had no family to borrow from, he had no money to buy the sacrificial items from the merchants.

There in the temple he made a vow not to let another Tabernacles pass without making this sacrifice. Afterward Jesus findeth him in the temple, and said unto him, Behold, thou art made whole: sin no more, lest a worse thing come unto thee. The man departed, and told the Jews that it was Jesus, which had made him whole. And therefore did the Jews persecute Jesus, and sought to slay him, because he had done these things on the sabbath day. But Jesus answered them, My Father worketh hitherto, and I work.

# Part II: Death

I Josiah, a Jew from the cursed city of Chorazin, had always believed that every man gets what he deserves in the end. God does not present himself as a fair God, but he is most definitely a righteous God. I had strayed away from that way of thinking for some time, but after attaining my healing my right mind returned.

Therefore, as I have said; all men are not treated equally, but they are all justly treated. Again, every man gets what he deserves in the end or so I believed. This was my motto until I found myself sentenced to be crucified upon a cross. Crucifixion, is the cruelest form of punishment under Roman law. It purposely inflicts a slow, public, painful death to the lawbreaker; so in fact death is the end of the law for the lawbreaker, but this punishment was purposed to inflict a shameful death. It serves as a vile, agonizing reminder to all, that to offend Roman law is to offend life. The sentenced soul is forced to carry the patibulum to the place of unification; the root and the branch unified in one. The condemned is usually ceremonially scourged, before he is made to bear the patibulum to his place of execution.

As I waited I remembered a day, before the end, when my mother placed her hand upon my heart and said something quick, something secret; she said something to better me, something that was in her heart. Something she had prayed about for some time. This is a practice of my people but if this practice has died out over the years, leave it that way, because before you can claim this type of healing I must make a disclaimer. You must never let the wrong person touch your heart! Be it in the flesh or spirit it is your heart, keep it safe. It is the way of men to have his son swear an oath to God before him, before his death. Again, the oath itself can be meaningful but if this tradition has died out over the years, do not revive it because oaths can be disastrous. As I hung there at the place of a skull awaiting death I could not help but look back at the day before and how it had completely gone wrong. I had gone to the temple to present a sacrifice for the good that was previously bestowed upon me; I swore to make this sacrifice before a year had passed and had intended to keep my vow, but I never got to see past the court of the gentiles.

The court of the gentiles is the area inside of the temple gates, but sits outside of the temple itself. This area was primarily a marketplace, with vendors selling souvenirs, sacrificial animals, food, as well as currency changers, that exchange Roman for Temple currency. There are also priests that serve as guides of the premises and also advise pilgrims on which sacrifices to present at the altar.

The gentiles truly have a place at and around the temple of God, but only a Jewish male could be shown inside the temple itself.

The temple itself is a vast, ornate, wonder of man. It sits as a magnificent crown, a dress upon the head of Jerusalem, a light that draws all men to the city of God. Peoples of every nation come to the temple to worship the one true God, Jehovah: its surrounds are compassed about with men and creatures from around the world.

Arabs, Libyans, Persians, Romans, Asians as well as rams, goats, oxen, asses and dromedaries all cry-out in their distinct dialects which results in a buzzing, overpowering, chaotic chatter. But, the walls of the temple are made of stones so dense that none of these sounds make it into the temple itself. There is chaos all around the city, but peace can be found within the temple walls. Slaves are sold in the city markets but bonds are loosed and prisoners freed within these confines. Upon entering the temple, the eyes are assailed as the ears were outside in the courtyard. When a man walks through the doors of the temple he may expect grandeur but what meets him is abundant grandeur. His vision is overwhelmed by the majesty, stateliness, and the glory of the inner house. The temple ceiling is like the sky but more true, the air fresher than earthly air, even the smoke from the fires is light upon the eyes. The glory of the house is blinding. I would tell you more about the temple but like I said before on this day I did not see the temple, therefore that description is for another day. I had spent the past year in various pursuits trying to gather the money needed to complete my vow, but I had no specific trade in which to rely on and there were many barriers to entry into my general fields of interest. I also had a temple fine that I had to pay for breaking Shabbat. Suffice it to say that, I did not have the money to buy the proper sacrifices as the moment came near; I made a deal with one of the sellers to work for him in exchange for the proper animals to present as a sacrifice. It pained me to work in this capacity because these sellers really were thieves; there was nothing fair about the rates they charged and their scales were unbalanced; all this evil was done in the house of God! It comforted me to know that this existence was only temporary; it was improbable but still possible for me to earn the money I needed to complete my vow. But the best plans of man must one day give way to the will of God. Jesus of Nazareth, had previously arrived in the city and was received as a King; palms and garbs covered the streets four days. Thereafter he arrived at the temple and began to cast out them that sold and bought in the temple, and overthrew the tables of the moneychangers, and the seats of them that sold doves. During the commotion myself and another took some of the money that fell from the tables and would have kept it but we were constrained.

There was quite a disruption in the temple because this Jesus would not suffer that any man should carry any vessel through the temple and said, "Is it not written, My house shall be called of all nations the house of prayer? but ye have made it a den of thieves." And the blind and the lame came to him in the temple; and he healed them. And when the chief priests and scribes saw the wonderful things that he did, and the children crying in the temple, and saying, "Hosanna to the Son of David." They were sore displeased, And said unto him, "hearest thou what these say?" And Jesus saith unto them, "Yeah have ye never read, Out of the mouth of babes and sucklings thou hast perfected praise?" But they took the truth of his word as blasphemy and sought how they might destroy him. When it was discovered that it was Jesus, that healed me at Bethesda and that I had been caught in the very act of stealing from the house of God, the priest sought a way to condemn Jesus with me. It did not help when one in the crowd said, "Jesus has the power to forgive sins, so if God will not condemn these men what right has a priest too?" This caused the chief priests and the elders of the people to demand of Jesus, "by what authority doest thou these things? and who gave thee this authority? " Jesus answered and said unto them, "I also will ask you one thing, which if ye tell me, I in like wise will tell you by what authority I do these things. The baptism of John, whence was it? from heaven, or of men?" And they reasoned with themselves, saying, If we shall say, From heaven; he will say unto us, Why did ye not then believe him? But if we shall say, Of men; we fear the people; for all hold John as a prophet. And they answered Jesus, and said, "We cannot tell." And he said unto them, "neither tell I you by what authority I do these things."

This man Jesus, had an unmatched knowledge of the law and was always far ahead of his accusers. He posed a question and said, "what think ye? A certain man had two sons; and he came to the first, and said, Son, go work to day in my vineyard. He answered and said, I will not: but afterward he repented, and went. And he came to the second, and said likewise. And he answered and said, I go, sir: and went not. Whether of them twain did the will of his father?" They say unto him, "the first." Jesus saith unto them, "verily I say unto you, That the publicans and the harlots go into the kingdom of God before you. For John came unto you in the way of righteousness, and ye believed him not: but the publicans and the harlots believed him: and ye, when ye had seen it, repented not afterward, that ye might believe him." At this saying, there was a cry for justice, repentance, and reformation throughout the temple. The priests deemed these cries as riotous, anti-roman, and disorderly conduct in the Lord's House. It was then that they took me away in bonds and went to find witnesses to accuse Jesus of Nazareth. I did not know it at the time but Jesus would be the catalyst which marked a 7 week period of time in which no man died upon the earth.

I was examined by some of the priests and was asked, "by what power doth this Nazarene do these things." "This man performs miracles," I said. "Who can do these things but God?" I was told that the other thief seized in the temple was witnessed assaulting and robbing a Roman citizen, who later died. (What more would you expect from a man of Bethsaida), I thought. My host said that it would be, could be assumed that I was in league with this thief and as therefore equally as guilty of the deed. I was told that if found guilty, I would most certainly be beaten and sentenced to death. The interrogator said, "Why face a certain painful death when you can save yourself by cooperating with us?" "There is no way I will bear false witness against any man, let alone one that does the willful work of God," I said. "This man has healed me and others. He has raised the dead and speaks with the wisdom and authority of God.

His words have power! He gives life; how can anyone seek his death?" I thought back to the many years I sat in agony by the pool of Bethesda waiting for the angel to trouble the water. I could not help but wonder if my past infirmity was due to the fact that in my future I would bear false witness against this just man and cause him to be sentenced to death. It was then I made up my mind that I would rather find death by telling the truth than life through lying lips.

Later that night I was told that I was to appear before the Sanhedrin. I was brought to the Chief Priest's house for a hearing. This was strange for several reasons; the Sanhedrin did not meet during festivals, they did not meet in homes, and they did not meet at night. I knew that none of these rules would be broken for a common thief like myself. I surmised that they wanted to hurriedly bring false accusation against Jesus, but because I did not study the law, I could not see the end of their logic. I entered the chamber and saw Jesus standing in silence before the council.

I myself witness several accusations against Jesus that I knew in my heart to be false from what I knew of this Jesus; all men know that God does not lie. From what I could tell, the main charges brought against him were blasphemy and breaking the commandments. One witness said that Jesus called himself the Son of God and had told his disciples to violate private property by going into a field on the sabbath and picking corn for him to eat. The accuser said that, when some of the Pharisees said unto the disciples, Why do ye that which is not lawful to do on the sabbath days? It was accused that, Jesus answered them by saying, if I choose to I will go into the house of God, and take and eat the shewbread, which is not lawful to eat but for the priests alone, but he could eat it because he was the Son of God and therefore, Lord also of the sabbath. I could not believe the level of half-truths and trickery implemented by the priests for even I knew that the code of Moses allowed for strangers to take food from a field that had been harvested. This led me to question their witness about the shewbread.

Another false witness accused Jesus of calling himself the King of the Jews and said that he would combine the Jews and the Gentiles and make one nation, one fold. He accused Jesus of saying that Jew and Gentile would be equal in the eyes of God and both receive Abraham's inheritance and the sure mercies of David.

When I saw the line of false witness against this just man I felt lost, but I heard one of the counsel say that these testimonies did not agree with previous testimonies. Apparently they had heard testimony for some time from different witnesses, even before Jesus had arrived. It was acknowledged by others that the witnesses did not agree; one of them said, "What are we accomplishing; here is this man performing many miraculous signs. If we let him go on like this, everyone will believe in him, and then the Romans will come and take away both our place and our nation." These words angered the High Priest and he said, "You know nothing at all! You do not realize that it is better for you that one man die for the people than that the whole nation perish." They believed that the people would rebel against the Romans in hopes of establishing a new Kingdom with Jesus as Lord. These men greatly feared the wrath of Rome and the loss of the powers given them by the Romans. Their true motives hung in the air, and there was silence for an uncomfortable length of time.In an attempt to voice my support of Jesus and seized the moment, I asked why the false witnesses were not punished as required in the law of Moses. I asked why the judges were not present for this questioning, but I was overshadowed by the High Priest saying, "This thief was in league with Jesus. He was caught stealing from the house of God, after this Jesus created a diversion by turning over tables of money and now this lawbreaker purposes to lecture us on the very codes he broke! Who is this Jesus to cause such turmoil by supposing to change the ordinances of the house of God? Who would cause confusion and disorder in God's house but the devil?" At that point I was sent out into the courtyard as the testimony continued. Truly what can a condemned man say for another, when his words speak to his own fate.

As I waited, I thought of Jesus and his predicament; it seemed as if the whole world was against this just man. In my mind I could still see him standing before the council; he stood erect and strait in his strength but he seemed to only be half there. He stood there a man clearly torn in two directions and between two worlds. He looked burdened as if he carried a great weight on his shoulders and seemed overjoyed to have lifted the great weight but this joy was mingled with heartache because he knew that so much depended upon him carrying this charge to the end. This mingled love shown by Jesus was enough to make me repent of my sins and beg God our Father for forgiveness; I repented in my heart. When I saw the Messiah being subject to such things I knew it to be the fulfillment of the law and prophets, but I wondered what kept the council from seeing this. I understood that so many hopes, and many more lives depended upon Jesus lifting this great burdensome debt on sin from off the shoulder of each man since Adam. Our beloved dead still carried this burden and therefore could not rest in peace. This clearly was the weight of the world upon the Son of God. But then as I came to this conclusion, there in the courtyard I recognized the man called Peter, that I had seen with Jesus.

And as he warmed himself by the fire, a maid saw him, and said unto them that were there, "This fellow was also with Jesus of Nazareth." I heard this man deny knowing Jesus with an oath he said, "I do not know the man." And after a while came unto him they that stood nearby, and said to Peter, "Surely thou also art one of them; for thy speech betrayeth thee." Then began Peter to curse and to swear, saying, "I know not the man." And immediately the cock crew. And after this he went out, and wept bitterly.

I could not judge Peter, but I took this to be an ominous sign when I remembered the words of the prophet. "Awake, O sword, against my shepherd, and against the man that is my fellow, saith the LORD of hosts: smite the shepherd, and the sheep shall be scattered: and I will turn mine hand upon the little ones. And it shall come to pass, that in all the land, saith the LORD, two parts therein shall be cut off and die; but the third shall be left therein. And I will bring the third part through the fire, and will refine them as silver is refined, and will try them as gold is tried: they shall call on my name, and I will hear them: I will say, It is my people: and they shall say, The LORD is my God."

I was taken back to my holding cell to await trial, sentencing, and death. I did not have to wait long because the night was already far spent. It seemed like mere moments before I was tried by Roman law and sentenced to be crucified. I was beaten by the soldiers of the court and forced to carry the patibulum to the execution point. As I was hoisted up to my final place of shame I felt at peace within myself mostly because I had no family to witness my disgrace, but wondered about the man Jesus.

Later, as I looked about I saw a man in the distance. He came upon the Tsent road beaten and true. He limped along the way to Golgotha with a cosmic train in his wake. I was distressed when I saw him bearing the entire cross, both pieces! This had never been done before! Myself and the world watched him fall several times before a man of great stature appeared to help him with his burden. As the man approached eyesight I could see that he was beaten and bruised so completely that I wondered what crime he had committed to deserve such chastisement and these many stripes. It was then I heard one of the soldiers announce, "

Behold Jesus of Nazareth, the King of the Jews." I jumped at the saying and almost uprooted my wooden post from the ground; I almost died of fear and disbelief when I saw what had been done to the Son of God and hoped to die before I saw more done and the cup of the wrath of God made to overflow. The soldiers disgracefully placed him between me and the other thief. I looked around and watched more intently for death than Job ever did.

Then Jesus said, "Father, forgive them; for they know not what they do," as the soldiers parted his raiment, and cast lots. And the people stood beholding. And the rulers also with them derided him, saying, He saved others; let him save himself, if he be Christ, the chosen of God. And the soldiers also mocked him, coming to him, and offering him vinegar, And saying, If thou be the king of the Jews, save thyself. And a superscription also was written over him in letters of Greek, and Latin, and Hebrew, THIS IS THE KING OF THE JEWS. Then the malefactor said, If thou be Christ, save thyself and us. But I rebuked him, and said, "Dost not thou fear God, seeing thou art in the same condemnation? And we indeed justly; for we receive the due reward of our deeds: but this man hath done nothing amiss." At that point I spoke aloud what had only been said and hoped for in my heart. "Lord, remember me when thou comest into thy kingdom." And Jesus said, "Verily I say unto thee, Today shalt thou be with me in paradise." He then looked to his mother and said, "Woman, behold, your son!" He then spoke as David and said, "My God, My God, why hast thou forsaken me?"

As his voice strained from exhaustion, pain, and dry anguish he said, "I thirst." Now there was set a vessel full of vinegar: and one of the soldiers filled a sponge with vinegar, and put it upon a reed with hyssop, and put it to his mouth. When Jesus therefore had received the vinegar, he said, "It is finished. Father, into thy hands

I commend my spirit:" and he bowed his head, and gave up the ghost. Now when the centurion saw what was done, he glorified God, saying, Certainly this was a righteous man. At that moment hell began to give up her dead and all manner of creatures were seen walking the earth. The soldiers almost ran for fear but stayed at their post from more abundant fear; they kept their duty but all wanted the process quickened. It was then that they broke my legs and those of the other thief. Damn it! I was crippled again, just as Jesus had warned me; the last clear thing I saw before I suffocated was a soldier take the spear of Africa and pierce the side of Jesus, and forthwith came there out blood and water.

It was revealed to me on the cross that God gave Jesus three commandments. (1) Be first in all things, be as God, and fulfill the law I spoke and the life of the prophets. (2) Become the doorway to reconcile My sheep to Me, the Shepherd, and usher them into the Sheepfold. (3) Lay down your life for the sheep and take your life up again, then return to Me and sit at My right hand until I make thy enemies thy footstool.

These are the truths I realized right before I died. Also, I finally understood how the woman was saved in childbearing. Death was passed through man but life through the woman. I would explain more but my time is up and as fluid filled my lungs and I could not speak I realized the truth of life; God gives every creature commandments, but only Jesus could keep his. Only Jesus could free us from the consequences of the commandments we broke, commandments given to us by God. Jesus, through obedience destroyed the curse which plagued every man since Adam because Jesus himself had no sin. I found life in the word of truth. I was so empowered by these truths that I almost came down off of the cross, not because I was somehow special, but only because that's how strong the desire was to tell somebody about who Jesus is. He came to earth God's Son in the form of a man, empowered by God himself to make peace between God and man by breaking the bond sin made between flesh and soul. Does not the word of God say, "For the word of God is quick, and powerful, and sharper than any two-edged sword, piercing even to the dividing asunder of soul and spirit, and of the joints and marrow, and is a discerner of the thoughts and intents of the heart." God told Adam, that on the day he ate of the tree he would surely die. On the day he disobeyed God, his soul was separated from the spirit of God. Satan came into the garden and separated us from the immortal spirit of God and had sewn the soul and flesh together. As God has said, "My spirit shall not always strive with man, for that he also is flesh: yet his days shall be an hundred and twenty years." But Jesus had come to give the souls life again not for the dead flesh. God truly does give life to the dying. Does not the word say that, "After that ye heard the word of truth, the gospel of your salvation: in whom also after that ye believed, ye were sealed with that holy Spirit of promise." This sealing is God's spirit returning to man, thus giving the dead souls life again. "All souls are mine the soul that sinneth, shall be a dead soul", A voice said, "And you, being dead in your sins and the uncircumcision of your flesh, hath he quickened together with him, having forgiven you all trespasses; Blotting out the handwriting of ordinances that was against us, which was contrary to us, and took it out of the way, nailing it to his cross; And having spoiled principalities and powers, he made a shew of them openly, triumphing over them in it. Let no man therefore judge you in meat, or in drink, or in respect of an holy day, or of the new moon, or of the sabbath days." I would enter paradise with a testimony.

But paradise would have to wait; I was quickened by Jesus and bought down from the cross to be with him. As it is written, "The first man Adam was made a living soul; the last Adam was made a quickening spirit." It seemed like but a moment, in the blink of an eye, but in that small window of time in which I floated between two worlds and was changed, a battle had been fought over the body and spirit of Jesus. I say this because I saw first hand the combatants and the results of the battle. Fallen angels and demons were set in array against God's Son: these made war with the Lamb, but were overcome by the Lamb: for he is Lord of lords, and King of kings: and they that are with him are called, and chosen, and faithful. On one side there was a mighty host of angels, on the other were fearsome minions terrible to look upon. But these devils lay broken and on their knees as the spirit of Jesus gave command. No, judged then commanded, their leader dictating the terms of their unconditional surrender. The body of Jesus had been taken away, do you know where the Lord's body was lain? I saw Death and Hell hand over two great keys to the two chosen ones of God, Enoch & Elijah for a time; the six other levels of Hell were to be opened. The spirit of Hell was taken away in chains and returned to his prison by an escort of angels. Death was loosed for a time and at this proclamation by Jesus, the dead returned to their state. Satan was not happy concerning this defeat but he too was freed for a season, however some of his soldiers were confined to the lower levels of hell, but such terms are for another time.

Oh yes, let me repeat: I entered paradise with a testimony.

Part III: Hell

(This is the better way to describe the abstract descent to hell)

I saw the end through the eyes of the last man

*I was the first-last man, and time passed so fast man
Jesus quickened me to see an earth that was sickly
Accelerated me to see things that must come quickly*

*The last man saw man's last days, gave man's last
praise Made sacrifice and presented it to cover our
ways*

Then before I returned, I blessed the Head of Days

*I'm the last man on earth There is no one besides me
There is only death beside me With a cruel smell
abiding*

*I am left to lament for myself I can only repent for
myself*

*Death has taken everyone else Atrocity covers
continents not cities There is no one to show pity*

Or judge the perpetrators with me No judges remain

So how can justice be attained

*Can anyone comprehend what I am saying? I have no
power to judge the dead*

*So I just grieve for them instead Until finality pains my
head*

Is one man's grief enough?

*A mass burial would be efficient But there is not earth
sufficient Should I just find a hole for myself?*

And let the dead just bury themselves

*Before the birds and rodents gorge themselves I put the
cares of the world behind me*

Still hoping that the Saints in paradise find me When I

die who will find me

Who will cry over the last man? When death has compassed the land

Who will console me on my death bed? And what will be said?

I'm the last man on earth There is no one besides me There is only death beside me

There is only one thing death can say to comfort me He will say what he always says

"I'm here for you"

When my life is forsaken

I will be taken to the other place

Does time and space end in this place My mouth with a bad taste

End with my head down in disgrace With my memories erased

I heard the truth and knew the truth

It ached sadly in my ear like a blue tooth It's not gospel if they can't say Jesus

If she can't say his name in every song it is wrong Then I remembered many times I was wrong

But God gave my heart a new song

It's not the gospel if they don't preach Jesus

If he can't profess Jesus, he does not possess Jesus Possess me and profess me to your Father, Jesus Its egregious and hell is ellacious

Dark, black, cruel, and so spacious

So spacious, it should be more spacious Don't fill it,

God let it be empty

*Then God said I can't be tempted so why tempt me
Please God exempt me, remove contempt from me
Because I did it all ignorantly*

*Your truth was still hidden from me But now that your
word is given to me*

I can go anywhere and be bidden of thee

Then I said who goes there, who goes with me

*And Jesus said, "I will never leave you nor forsake
you" I'm taking you to paradise because you chose me*

*I chose you, fill you, compose you Justify you, just don't
defy me*

*Confess and try me and you will never be outside my
body Disembodied, Disjointed, heaven is my abode,
just join it Be anointed and death you can forever
disappoint it*

*We went further down into cursed ground Cursed is he
for our sakes he was staked*

*He was beaten and wounded his life too soon ended He
hung from a tree before he saved me*

Thank you God for the gift you gave me

*I repented as we descended grace ended Hell is the
worst place*

*I don't wanna take first place in this place Jesus said
be advised to run to win the race And you won't end up
here in the first place It's a race keep the faith, keep the
pace Quickly take the Help of God from heaven*

Add leaven for Taste leave this place, make HASTE!

When we arrived in Paradise I was quite caught by surprise. I discovered that all Jews that had kept the commandments from the beginning were in Paradise. I am assuming you know that Adam and Eve were given commands to keep, it was not just Moses that received commandments from God. I will also assume that you know that any male child that is not circumcised on the eighth day, that soul is cutoff from the Jewish congregation because he has broken the covenant. As I said before every man is given commandments to keep! Adversely, all of the gentiles that had died since the beginning were carried over the burning gulf into the other place, a place of sorrow!

Now, Satan had pretended to be God, he had done this since the first man's arrival and had all but convinced most of the Jews in paradise that they were in heaven already and that no further sacrifice was required on their part. Satan even went as far as to teach those that believed in him his counterfeit doctrine, which included the worshiping of Saints, which is idolatry. Most of the Jews there had no memory of their former lives on earth, but all those souls in the other place remembered their sinful existence on earth all too well and paid for their misdeeds. A few chosen Jews were allowed by Jehovah God to keep their memories; the others were free to fulfill every immediate imagination they could fabricate while sinfully enjoying the pleasures of the flesh. In paradise every sense was increased until no man could limit his desires; the Jews lustfully served their imaginations. This servitude became a perpetual form of presumed, sanctioned idolatry. I say sanctioned because Satan had convinced most of them that sin no longer had a hold on them because they were in paradise; Satan wrote and enforced the law of paradise and the only recognized sin for a man was not relying on him to fulfill their every desire. Satan assured everyone that the test of the world was complete; there a man could reap the rewards of his labors. In many ways it made sense because the Jews are God's chosen people; they are promised eternal joy, and the realization of their desire for justice upon their enemies. In their minds they had to be in heaven because they could clearly see that the Gentiles were in hell.

I was commanded to speak to all times in all tenses. I would speak first to Two and Twenty of the Patriarchs, which through predestination had kept themselves from being deceived by Satan. I was told that I would need to hear the testimony of these elders to come to understand the fullness of my own. I was told that I would be sent to do a work in this place. As was befitting, I would speak with Adam first.

Adam had kept himself in all the ways of God: Adam knew that this "Paradise" was merely a time of grace. He viewed paradise as another garden of Eden and had determined within himself that he would not repeat the mistakes of the past. He knew the voice of God and because of this he knew that the Deceiver did not speak as God. Adam vowed long ago that he would listen to no other voice but God's. He knew full well that through disobedience he had brought sin into the world and passed it on to all men, all his seed. Through much hope Adam waited for the Messiah to come and take away the stain of sin from man. As he watched his sons in paradise he saw them sinning mightily just as they had done on the earth. Adam knew the commandment of God, that he cannot tolerate sin and therefore knew that Satan was subtly trying to fool mankind again.

Wherefore, as by one man sin entered into the world, and death by sin; and so death passed upon all men, for that all have sinned: For until the law sin was in the world: but sin is not imputed when there is no law. However, there is no judgment where there is no sin, but because of sin death reigned in judgment. This judgment was not final but, nevertheless death reigned from Adam to Moses, even over them that had not sinned after the similitude of Adam's transgression, who is the figure of him that was to come. But not as the offence, so also is the free gift. For if through the offence of one many be dead, much more the grace of God, and the gift by grace, which is by one man, Jesus Christ, hath abounded unto many. And not as it was by one that sinned, so is the gift: for the judgment was by one to condemnation, but the free gift is of many offences unto justification. For if by one man's offence death reigned by one; much more they which receive abundance of grace and of the gift of righteousness shall reign in life by one, Jesus Christ. Therefore as by the offence of one judgment came upon all men to condemnation; even so by the righteousness of one the free gift came upon all men unto justification of life. For as by one man's disobedience many were made sinners, so by the obedience of one shall many be made righteous. Moreover the law entered, that the offence might abound. But where sin abounded, grace did much more abound: That as sin hath reigned unto death, even so might grace reign through righteousness unto eternal life by Jesus Christ our Lord.

Adam spoke plainly to me and said, "To continue in sin is to continue living outside of God's will." The Jews in paradise were in that very state!

Abel had kept himself in all the ways of God: he came to know first hand that God himself hears the voice of the slain through the blood. Abel's blood had petitioned God for justice when his brother Cain slew him. Abel by experience knew that if the cries of his imperfect blood were heard and heeded from heaven to the curse, how better the petitioning of the Son of God's precious blood would work to man's salvation. Under the old covenant all men were murders in the semblance of Cain. The word of life is spoken through the voice of the blood and it is through the unblemished blood of Jesus that we are reconciled with God. Abel explained to me that, Perfect love casts out all sin. In a manner of speaking, (we were infected by sin and Jesus cured us through his blood; the well of our blood was changed thus purging the infection). The holy and pure blood of Jesus surfaced in the garden where Jesus resisted unto blood, striving against sin knowing full well that no sin sacrifice is offered without blood. Jesus Christ banished the stain of sin from mankind through his sacrifice on the cross and is now become the mediator of the new covenant. If Jesus is our Lord, then we are covered by his blood under the New Testament; his blood speaking better things toward man than that of Abel's.

We now as believers have no reason to fear death, because we have been fully reconciled with God and reside within the general assembly; we are now members of the family of God. I say this because "blood" also means, "family". We are therefore adopted by blood and have become sons of God; sons that no longer die as men, but live forever as children of God. Our blood speaks in testimony to the adoption as we cry, Abba, Father. I marveled at how one with such brief a life understood the mystery of Jesus.

Seth had kept himself in all the ways of God: he viewed the fall of man and the death of Abel not only as tragic events but events caused by the same reason. There was a lack of love in both cases; if his parents had loved God they would have kept his commands and if Cain knew brotherly love he would not have murdered Abel. We are all sons of Adam & Eve but Seth benefited more than any other because he was raised by them after they had learned from the mistakes made with Cain and Abel. Reared by loving parents and watched over by all of creation Seth came to know the voice of God from an early age. The song of Seth's heart focused more with brotherly love, because he had lost both of his brothers tragically. Most of the commandments men receive deal with brotherly love. Seth relayed to me that there was no greater form of brotherly love than that which Jesus showed. Jesus so quickly perfected love because love is of God. He said, "Beloved, let us love one another: for love is of God; and every one that loveth is born of God, and knoweth God. He that loveth not knoweth not God; for God is love. In this was manifested the love of God toward us, because that God sent his only begotten Son into the world, that we might live through him. Herein is love, not that we loved God, but that he loved us, and sent his Son to be the propitiation for our sins. Beloved, if God so loved us, we ought also to love one another. We ought to love and be-loved" I agreed with Seth and acknowledged the spirit of truth in these words, they can only be attributed to God. God is Love therefore Love must be preeminent in the heart of every servant of God. The Jews in paradise did not regard Love as preeminent. They did not love God because they could not recognize God or know who God is. God has a place in the soul of every believer, but the Jews of paradise needed to be introduced to God.

For this purpose Jesus was sent to paradise and preached peace to the Jews of Paradise. If they believed in Jesus, as the son of God, and called upon his name, he would save them from all sin and introduce them to God, the Father. For whosoever shall call upon the name of the Lord shall be saved. But they could not call on him in whom they have not believed. They could not believe in him of whom they have not heard, and could not hear without a preacher. And the preacher could not preach, except he be sent.

And the preacher could not preach, except he be sent? It is important to realize here that the Patriarchs in Paradise still had their memories and knew all too well who God is, but they could not preach, because they were not sent to Paradise to preach. Let those who are wise hear, let the scribe record this truth forever. Where is the wise? Where is the scribe? Where is the disputer of this world?

Hath not God made foolish the wisdom of this world? For after that in the wisdom of God the world by wisdom knew not God, it pleased God by the foolishness of preaching to save them that believe.

The Jews in paradise also chose to wrongly reveled in the punishment given their enemies and would never even consider them as brothers. Seth watched many gentiles endure countless torments through the cruel implements of Hell and would not dare consider himself to be in heaven with so much heartache so near!

Noah had kept himself in all the ways of God: he had kept God's command and built the ark to house the chosen of God and by doing so had saved himself and his family alive. Never before had every living creature that creepeth been gathered together in one place. It was revealed to Noah that God had a number predestined of him to be saved, even the animals knew this. And some who thought themselves saved were merely given a dispensation of grace only to be sacrificed later. Have you not heard of how the clean animals were taken into the ark in sevens and how in sevens they survived the flood, but one of each was sacrificed to God by Noah after the flood, thus leaving three pairs! Noah understood this to be a sign of things to come. He knew that God would gather in one place all the things that are in him; all things that are made clean and would save them from the coming storm. To be caught outside of the ark of safety is to die. Noah had witnessed the vengeance of God once before upon sinful men who lusted after every imagination of their hearts. Noah knew imaginations to be a sect of demons which feed upon the lusts of man and therefore would not serve these demons. Noah saw the people of his day succumb to the imaginations of their heart until their every thought became evil. He knew that God demanded that his servants be clean; he also knew that this cleanness could not come through works. This cleanliness could only come through the sacred blood of the Messiah, Jesus Christ.

The Jews in paradise also served these imaginations and therefore remained in sin. Noah knew that this sin of idolatry would not stand and because of this sin, this "paradise" would soon be destroyed.

Abraham had kept himself in all the ways of God: he had recognized God as his shield and his exceedingly great reward.

Abraham knew that in order to receive his reward and to be shielded all around by God, he had to believe God, obey God, and be found worthy of God's rewards. Abraham had also recognized Melchizedek as a priest forever of the most high God and had paid tithes to Melchizedek of all of his substance after destroying the kings. When these two met there was represented a prophet in Abraham and a Priest and King in Melchizedek; this was done to foreshadow the appearance of Jesus Christ, who would come in the perfection of all three; Prophet, Priest, and King. Abraham waited for the appearance of Jesus who would come to fulfill the office of Melchizedek. Jesus would come as an eternal priest to offer up himself as a lamb on the altar, a sacrifice for the sins of the world. He came as the lamb that took Isaac's place when Abraham would have sacrificed him up.

The promise was made to Abraham and his seed; this promise of inheriting the Promised Land was both physical and spiritual. The faith of Abraham had been counted for righteousness and therefore the faith of his seed in Jesus is counted for righteousness and opens the door of admittance into heaven, the spiritual Promised Land.

God had told Abram, a son of Adam, to depart from the house of his father and go into a land he was to be shown. As spiritual sons of Abraham we are to depart from earth, the land of our fathers and be gathered in heaven, the land of promise. No man can enter heaven without being approved by Jesus, therefore any man which desire to be shielded all around by the blood of Jesus must first believe and accept the testimony of God concerning Jesus, obey God, and be found worthy of this reward.

Issac had kept himself in all the ways of God: he knew by experience that his father walked in hope and obeyed God without question. Abraham showed his son Issac that if a man of God is faithful, that God in turn will be faithful. Abraham testified to Issac concerning how God saved Lott and his house because of Abraham's faithfulness and relationship with God. God had promised Abraham, that the world would be blessed through his seed thus prophesying the birth, death, and resurrection of the Messiah. Issac was a child of miracle birth therefore his very existence left no room for doubting God's word. There is no room for doubt in the heart of any servant of God. Issac clearly recalled the day in which his father placed the wood for an offering to God upon his back; he was made to carry it to the place of sacrifice. As he lay on the altar Issac waited in hope and expectation for the lamb, that would be offered to God in his stead for a sin sacrifice, which foreshadowed the death of Jesus.

Did not Jesus bare his wooden cross and die in our stead? God truly did provide a lamb of salvation when death was all but certain.

The lessons of Issac's later years also stayed with him. He knew that sometimes a man's sight fails him therefore a man of God has to recognize the voice which speaks to him. Issac did not bless the son he intended to bless at first but he did recognize the chosen son's voice upon hearing it. Issac told me plainly that you have to know for yourself who speaks to you, and once you know don't be fooled by your earthly senses. Issac said that to truly know a thing is of God.

Esau was more concerned about filling his stomach with pottage than over his birthright and Issac was beguiled through his want of savory meats. Issac declared to me that a man's stomach should not be allowed to have everything it craves; a man of God must control all cravings and the only thing a man of God should crave at the end of life is to see the face of Jesus because it is Jesus that will keep him and his family after he passes. A man may bless his sons and make preparation for his death all he pleases, but the day will come when he will have to leave all that he has in God's hands. The Jews of paradise found themselves in the wrong hands.

Jacob had kept himself in all the ways of God: he had wrestled God and had seen God face to face. Jacob witnessed a ladder that reached from earth to heaven and had seen messengers of God going up and down thereon entering into God's rest. Jacob as heir to the promise had been pushed towards its delivery and had himself seen his children herded towards its realization, but he also knew that the earthly promised land was not the eternal place of rest. He assured me that the eternal place of rest is at the end of the ladder he saw reaching up into heaven and only the spiritual son's of Abraham can reach it; those sons that believed God and accepted him as Abraham did; not those that wrestled with God as Israel did.

Jacob become heir to the promise over his brother Esau, because Esau despised his birthright and did not value it. He knew the end of such a man would be weeping, and bitter tears. Jacob knew that the Jews could not please God because they were themselves children of expectation and not keepers of the promise. Those Jews that did not circumcise their bodies on the eighth day were excluded forever from the congregation, likewise any man that did not circumcise his heart by having the mind of Christ would suffer the same fate.

Jacob observed the Jews in paradise and knew from their actions that they still had not entered the true place of rest. God rested from all his works on the seventh day and man will have to rest from all his works also before he can enter into God's rest. The Jews of paradise were farther away from this rest than they had ever been because they sinned more than ever before.

God had blessed Jacob and had given him a new name as a sign of his favor and power with God. Jacob waited for the day when all of his sons would be given new names and shown favor with God.

There is a new name waiting for those who rest from iniquity, those that harden not their hearts when the call is heard. There is a new name waiting for those that accept Christ as Lord and Savior.

Joseph had kept himself in all the ways of God: he faithfully believed that all things belong to God and proceed forth from the mouth of God. He was faithful because he believed the things God showed him and kept himself on the way to the fulfillment of the vision. He himself told pharaoh that several dreams were one vision, because God has a singular vision for each of our lives; it is also God that owns the interpretation of each man's vision. It is not for one man to speak over another man's life unless it is to ask a blessing from God. Did not Jacob bless pharaoh?

Joseph's brothers attempted to kill the dreamer to destroy the dream, but even in envy they could not change the vision God had for Joseph's life, which spoke to preserve life. Joseph later told his brothers that, "Now therefore be not grieved, nor angry with yourselves, that ye sold me hither: for God did send me before you to preserve life. For these two years hath the famine been in the land: and yet there are five years, in the which there shall neither be earing nor harvest. And God sent me before you to preserve you a posterity in the earth, and to save your lives by a great deliverance.

So now it was not you that sent me hither, but God: and he hath made me a father to Pharaoh, and lord of all his house, and a ruler throughout all the land of Egypt."

When Joseph had power enough to exact retribution from his brothern he did not. He knew that his station was to preserve life; Joseph had a vision, a purpose, and he continually walked in that purpose. The Jews of paradise had no faith, no vision, and no purpose.

Moses had kept himself in all the ways of God:
Moses received God's commands but knew Israel to be too rebellious and stiff-necked to keep them. He also knew that the sins they committed could not be cleansed without blood. Moses called for heaven and earth to bear record against the children of Israel; God wrote a song as a reminder to them of the covenant they accepted. The Jews were commanded to teach this song to their children and to never forget it. Moses said, "Now seeing that they are compassed about with so great a cloud of witnesses, Israel should have lain aside every weight, and sin; Looking unto Jesus the author and finisher of our faith; who for the joy that was set before him endured the cross, despising the shame, and is set down at the right hand of the throne of God." This sacrifice is enough to save everyone that believes; if any man were in the end lost, they would have no excuse. This song that was commanded to their memory was taught to all by the Patriarchs, however this song was never sung because the people did not have true joy. Satan used their loss of memory as a means to corrupt them; he led astray many of the Jews. God had promised to break his covenant when the Jews left to serve other gods, but this knowledge in itself did not deter Israel. Moses revealed to me that Jesus would only appear to those who seek him and wait for his appearance, just as God does. Moses waited on the Son of God to issue a new covenant and cleanse the people of God with his blood, just as Moses himself had sprinkled those who accepted the old covenant. As it is written

of Moses, "And he took the book of the covenant, and read in the audience of the people: and they said, All that the LORD hath said will we do, and be obedient. And Moses took the blood, and sprinkled it on the people, and said, Behold the blood of the covenant, which the LORD hath made with you concerning all these words."

To enact the old covenant the people first heard the word and then confessed God as the mediator of the covenant. Moses knew that the only way for anyone to be completely redeemed is by accepting and confessing openly Jesus, the Son of God, as High Priest and mediator of the new covenant. The new covenant was enacted because the old was flawed in that man could not be free completely of sin. As said before there is no remission of sins without blood therefore the death of Jesus was necessary for our restoration. The resurrection of Jesus was also by necessity for him to serve as High Priest to mediate for man. Under the new covenant, Jesus intercedes for man in heaven before God himself as our High Priest and cleanses us eternally with his pure blood.

Aaron had kept himself in all the ways of God: he was the brother of Moses and the first High Priest of Israel. God had blessed him with eloquent speech, so when it came to dealing with Pharaoh and the Israelites, he spoke for Moses, as his prophet. God had chosen to show Pharaoh his power by making Moses seem like a god and by making Aaron his prophet.

The gods the Egyptians worshiped were stone statues but Moses was alive and even his prophet had great power. As a god Moses did not speak directly to Pharaoh, therefore the better orator, Aaron, spoke with Pharaoh. In this way Aaron saw first hand how someone who is not God could appear to be God to a non-believer. Those without the purest form of faith, that is true faith, can be fooled because they do not have a relationship with God. They can be deceived because they choose to believe that a creation can be

God.

Later in life Aaron learned by experience not to bend to the will of the majority by giving the people the desires of their heart, because there desire is evil continually; Israel was in the presence of the living God, but asked not to have a relationship with God, instead they begged Aaron to make a golden calf, that they might worship it. Aaron saw this same thing happening in paradise; the people did not know God, but worshiped Satan in the image of God because he gave them the desires of their heart. Aaron knew that God would not give the people all of the desires of their heart, because their hearts were evil continually. Aaron acknowledged that the truest desire or expectation of the creature is to be saved from sin. He knew that the Messiah would come in the similitude of Moses to deliver the people from the land of sin and sin.

Joshua had kept himself in all the ways of God: he was strong and courageous in his faith towards God. He led the armies of God to victory after victory and to their ultimate goal of conquering the promised land. Joshua learned the importance of obeying God through the punishments given the rebellious Israelites who questioned and murmured against God time after time; he learned from the mistake made by Aaron and Moses which caused them not to be allowed admittance into the promised land. He learned that God's commands must be followed to the letter.

Joshua was not born a prince nor by birthright did he inherit a position of leadership but he proved himself a leader by answering the call each and every time a man was needed to represent God; Joshua would quickly volunteer to uphold the banner of God and act as his emissary. Because Joshua upheld the holy banner of God, God listened to Joshua when he asked God to hold the sun and moon still during a battle so that he could finish the battle in daylight. There was no day like that before it nor after it in which

God listened to a man's voice, but Jesus commanded all these things to prove himself as God. Have you not heard how the men marvelled concerning Jesus, saying, "What manner of man is this, that even the winds and the sea obey him!" God is always available to his children when they call upon him for aid. God fought for Israel and Joshua knew that through obedience and faith that God would always redeem Israel.

Joshua was there when Moses redeemed Israel from the sting of Egyptian whips and loosed the people from their bonds. He had come to see that the Jews of paradise were still in bondage; sin and dismissal from the congregation had taken the place of the Egyptian whips and death. Joshua looked upon the faithlessness and idolatry of the Jews in paradise and knew that their rebellious nature had followed them into paradise. He knew that God would not allow this type of man into heaven, the land of promise.

Caleb had kept himself in all the ways of God: when ten spies returned from the land of Canaan with an evil report, only Joshua and Caleb believed in God enough to prophesy Israel's conquest of the land. The ten spies believed that the giants of the land could not be beaten by the armies of God; their evil report put fear into the hearts of the people of Israel and caused them to disobey God by refusing to enter the promised land. Because of this God made them to wander the desert forty years until all the adult Israelites died except Joshua and Caleb.

Caleb believed God to be faithful and acted by faith and was not possessed by the spirit of fear as the ten spies were. God himself testified of Caleb, "But my servant Caleb, because he had another spirit with him, and hath followed me fully, him will I bring into the land whereinto he went and his seed shall possess it." Caleb entered the promised land because he believed God, and followed

God fully with his whole heart. Caleb loved God with his whole heart therefore there was no room for fear in his heart; perfect love casteth out all fear. Those who enter heaven must do the same. They must not have the spirit of the world, but must be filled with the spirit of God.

The spirit of the world brings grief, punishment, and promised death, but the spirit of God brings joy and eternal life. Caleb declared to me that he had searched this land of paradise and knew completely in his heart that this was not heaven; paradise is not the land of promise.

Deborah had kept herself in all the ways of God: she was a prophetess and judge over Israel after Ehud died. There was a godly spirit about her and due to this I could see how she inspired Barak to take ten-thousand men and go up and fight the host of Canaan's iron chariots. Deborah was a great motivator and spoke positively of people. Due to her status with God, she was a light to Israel, and guide to Barak; he viewed her as having great favor with God, and relied on her heavily because of this. She prophesied Israel's victory over Cannan, but even then, Barak, would not go to war without her with him. Deborah found a woman to be just as effective as a man when it came to doing the work of the Lord. She herself was a great judge over Israel and in the process of performing God's office she also prophesied, the head of Canaan's army, Sisera's death at the hands of a woman.

Deborah observed the Jews of paradise and knew that they would come into judgment for their sins and acts against the ways of God. Deborah marveled because in all her years in paradise the Jews of paradise had never sang a song to the glory of God. How could there be paradise without praise? She counted this spirit which opposed God as the real enemy and those overpowered by this spirit were casualties of war. She spoke against the enemies of God and said, "So let all thine enemies perish, O Lord: but let them that love him be as the sun when he goeth forth in his might." This was a prophecy of the coming of Jesus. Deborah and the other Patriarchs were a light for me; their testimonies were a light and a fire within me, which helped to kindle the truth within me.

Gideon had kept himself in all the ways of God: he was unsure of himself and his calling but he always answered the call. God realized that, because Israel had served other gods for so long that, he had to reintroduce himself to Gideon and Israel. He allowed Gideon to test and prove him as God. This was done so that Gideon could confirm by his own methods that God truly spoke to him and that He is all powerful. Gideon was commanded by God to destroy the idols of his father and turn away from worshiping false gods.

Israel had turned away from God and God wanted Israel to see that if they kept the faith, the multitudes of their enemies could not overwhelm them or rule over them. God accomplished this by sending Gideon and 300 men to face an army comprised of several different nations. God told Gideon that he wanted the glory of the victory, God wanted to restore Israel's faith in him as the one true God. They needed to see that superior numbers did not matter, because God is all powerful and superior to the false gods of the heathens. Israel was made to realize that, if God is for you, men can't stand against you. Gideon took 300 men to face an army of over one hundred thousand soldiers, but even with vastly superior numbers his enemies were afraid because they knew that the Lord was with Gideon; the heathen revered God more than the Israelites did. They feared the sword of the Lord and Gideon, which became Israel's battle rally. I was taken back by how the heathen believed and feared God in the Old Testament, but saw God as the God of Israel only. They did not see him as a God over all, even though they viewed him as having great power they did not feel that they had a right to accept God as their God. They did not see him as being available to all. The arrival of Jesus as Messiah ushered in a new age in which all men could claim a right to the God of Israel as their God and his son, Jesus, as their Savior. The gentiles could finally live peaceably with the Jews side by side in the promised land.

Job had kept himself in all the ways of God: he was a faithful servant and believed that he would see Jesus in the flesh. Job had suffered and endured much loss in fact he lost more than any man before him except Adam, but even after losing all that he had he still worshiped God. Job said, "Naked came I out of my mother's womb, and naked shall I return thither: the LORD gave, and the LORD hath taken away; blessed be the name of the LORD." Because of his faith Job did not sin or charge God foolishly. He knew that to whom much is given much is required and that a servant of God must except good and evil at the hand of God. After losing everything and in the midst of agony Job said, "Though he slay me, yet will I trust in him." I marveled at the faith of Job because his status in the eyes of man did not concern him; his wife and three great friends all told Job that his sufferings were due to sin, but Job kept his integrity because he acknowledged that all men sin, therefore whatever sufferings he experienced were not only because of sin, but more-so because it was allowed by God. Job examined his state completely and many times proclaimed that it would have been better for him not to be born than to be abandoned by God. All that he loved had died but Job believed that he would regain all that he lost on earth upon entering heaven. He did not hope for death or fear it but saw death as a necessary step towards an eternity with God. Job knew himself to be a servant of the everlasting God, who is the righteous judge, and that his earthly existence however troubled was only a flicker in the eternal flame of his God given spirit; Job knew that his spiritual relationship with God would continue after death. Job viewed his faith in God and his eternal relationship in the spirit with God to be more important than his earthly existence, family, friendships, riches, or well-being. Did not Jesus say, "And every one that hath forsaken houses, or brethren, or sisters, or father, or mother, or wife, or children, or lands, for my name's sake, shall receive an hundredfold, and shall inherit everlasting life." Job knew himself to be an eternal servant first and foremost and he served God without preconditions. Job refused to turn away from God and said, "All the days of my appointed time will I wait, Till my change come." He had a relationship with God and knew God for himself; Job had to know God in order to be able to wait on God.

How can anyone wait on God if they do not believe in God, or please the true God if they have not heard of God, and how can they hear without being appointed to hear, and who can appoint times but God?

Not only did he wait on God in life but Job also knew that there would be a grace period after death in which he would have to wait on his Redeemer; Job waited expectantly on the Messiah in paradise and prophesied of the resurrection and said, "For I know that my Redeemer liveth, and that he shall stand at the latter day upon the earth." Of the ascension he further said, "Also now, behold my witness is in heaven, And my record is on high." Job realized the importance of Christ and acknowledged that one cannot hope to see heaven without believing in Jesus. Job's testimony also shows us that we must forgive those that wrong us if we hope to be blessed by God and live righteously as servants of Jesus Christ. God restored all that Job had lost because Job quickly repented of his sins and prayed for his friends even though they accused him falsely. God blessed Job with twice the possessions he had before and gave him ten more children to comfort him of the ten children he had lost. So the Lord blessed the latter end of Job more than his beginning.

Hannah had kept herself in all the ways of God: she came boldly before the altar and petitioned God for a son. As a godly woman she recognized God as being all powerful by believing that God was able to answer her request and honored God by promising the child to God even before she was with child. I marked the fact that a barren woman promised a child to God's service before she became pregnant. Hannah had bore a burden of shame because her husband had two wives, he had children from her rival, but Hannah herself was barren. Hannah refused to allow the enemy the pleasure of making her fret, she approached God with the very thing the enemy attacked her about. In the midst of anguish, she poured out her heart to God through faith, hoping with expectation. In exchange for a son she promised to lend him back to the Lord all the days of his life. She testified that not only must a price be paid when we are blessed by God, but we are made to know up front that we have an obligation to God. Some blessings are withheld because people will not acknowledge the obligation, which is kin to oblation. When we make a petition to God we must be willing to do what's right in the eyes of the Lord if we truly expect the request to be granted; we must also keep our end of the bargain. The son she received was purchased with a price, Hannah realized that the Messiah would purchase all of us for a price, and once bought we would not be free to follow after earthly desires, because before we were purchased we were dedicated to God. Of Jesus she said, "He will keep the feet of his saints, and the wicked shall be silent in darkness; for by strength shall no man prevail. The adversaries of the LORD shall be broken to pieces; out of heaven shall he thunder upon them: the LORD shall judge the ends of the earth; and he shall give strength unto his king, and exalt the horn of his anointed." She spoke of the ressurection when she said, "He shall give strength unto his King and exalt the horn of his anointed." Hannah spoke of the blood of Jesus when she said, "for by strength shall no man prevail."

Hannah knew that if she honored God first that he would honor her, and God did honor her by blessing her with five more children after Samuel. She further praised God after Samuel was born by saying, "My heart rejoiceth in the LORD, mine horn is exalted in the LORD: my mouth is enlarged over mine enemies; because I rejoice in thy salvation. There is none holy as the LORD: for there is none beside thee: neither is there any rock like our God. Talk no more so exceeding proudly; let not arrogancy come out of your mouth: for the LORD is a God of knowledge, and by him actions are weighed." Let's examine her actions: Hannah could have prayed at home but she sought God at the temple and prayed hoping to be proved a goodly wife by providing her husband, Elkanah, with a son. Her mind was on God first and then her husband; Hannah was truly a godly woman.

Eli had kept himself in all the ways of God: he served in the temple of God and performed his duty as a priest. As he served he inspired many in the process of performing his duty. Eli encouraged Hannah and later mentored Samuel in the ways of God. When describing the will of God, Eli, told Samuel, "It is the LORD: let him do what seemeth him good." He believed with all his heart that God does as he pleases and that as men we shouldn't put anything before God. Eli came to believe this because his sons sinned against God and were punished because of it. His sons did not walk in the ways of God because they profaned the offerings, which made the people abhor sacrificing to God. Because of this God told Eli, "I said indeed that thy house, and the house of thy father, should walk before me for ever: but now the LORD saith, Be it far from me; for them that honour me I will honour, and they that despise me shall be lightly esteemed." A similar judgment was later enacted against Israel. This judgment against his house caused Eli to realize that God desired a priest that would walk perfectly before him forever.

God desired a priest that would honour him; Eli realized that only the

Messiah could accomplish this. To establish this God himself said, "This is my beloved Son, in whom I am well pleased; hear ye him." Jesus himself said, "I can of mine own self do nothing: as I hear, I judge: and my judgment is just; because I seek not mine own will, but the will of the Father which hath sent me." Eli of all people knew the importance of a son seeking his father's will and working to please him. We are to please the Father and should honour God in all that we do.

Eli's great failure in life was his inability to control his sons, which made Israel to sin. In paradise Eli witnessed the same disregard to the ways of God and hoped for the appearing of the Messiah.

Samuel had kept himself in all the ways of God: he knew that without the shedding of blood there can be no remission of sins, but came to know that obedience is better than sacrifice. He told me of how the scape goat had to be sacrificed repeatedly because man in his own wisdom chose not to obey the voice of God. The blood of bulls and goats did indeed purify the flesh for a time, but these sacrifices were not perfect and could not remove sin entirely, therefore the sacrifice was made repeatedly. The sacrifice was made yearly by the high priest but Samuel had looked to a day when the precious, perfect blood of Jesus would be sacrificed once for the past and future sins of many. This gift was left through the testament of Jesus Christ to be received upon the sinners confession of Jesus as the Son of God and belief that God raised Christ from the dead.

The gift of the covering of the blood of Jesus would hide all sin

ascribed to the believer. For if the blood of bulls and of goats, and the ashes of an heifer sprinkling the unclean, sanctifieth to the purifying of the flesh: How much more shall the blood of Christ, who through the eternal Spirit offered himself without spot to God, purge your conscience from dead works to serve the living God?

The blood of Jesus unlike that of the scapegoats was pure to the eternal covering of the believer. Samuel had seen Saul's sin of pride and his foolish belief that God accepted sacrifice in exchange for obedience. As Samuel told Saul, "Hath the LORD as great delight in burnt offerings and sacrifices, as in obeying the voice of the LORD? Behold, to obey is better than sacrifice, and to hearken than the fat of rams. For rebellion is as the sin of witchcraft, and stubbornness is as iniquity and idolatry. Because thou hast rejected the word of the LORD, he hath also rejected thee from being king." Disobedience leads to rejection by God and separation.

It is important to note that the body of Christ is composed of believers and the blood of Christ is not only covering the believer but it is also pumped through his veins by his heart if he has the mind of Christ. There is no reason to ingest the blood of Christ when wine is commanded. Jesus changed water to wine and then wine to blood, but on the cross out came blood and water, which only left wine to speak to his commandments; the commandments of confession, belief, and baptism. There was no body nor blood left behind therefore Christ left bread and wine to be used in remembrance of him, not that the bread and wine should take the place of his body and blood, and the sacrifice be made continual, but that his charge be kept by obedience in observing The Holy Communion. The Lord's Supper is kept so that in it obedience should abound not that the sacrifice should abound. The blood sacrifice is made once unto death but by it the grace of God abounds through its covering which gives life and abides continually.

David had kept himself in all the ways of God: he passionately refused to stretch forth his hand against God's anointed. The Jews did not follow his example because if they had they never would have crucified, Jesus, the Messiah. David spared Saul's life twice when Saul was delivered into his hand and said, "The LORD render to every man his righteousness and his faithfulness: for the LORD delivered thee into my hand to day, but I would not stretch forth mine hand against the LORD'S anointed.

And, behold, as thy life was much set by this day in mine eyes, so let my life be much set by in the eyes of the LORD, and let him deliver me out of all tribulation." Because David believed that God was faithful to keep his word and fight his battles for him, even his enemies had to recognized this. Then Saul said to David, "Blessed be thou, my son David: thou shalt both do great things, and also shalt still prevail." By this Saul confirmed what was already in David's heart.

David, believed God was faithful and able to keep his word by making him king, even against the desires of his enemies. He walked by faith boldly and faced whatever challenge presented itself against him or Jehovah God; he faced a giant in Goliath because he dared defy the army of God. David was also pursued by armies composed of enemies, countrymen, and family. There was much adversity in the life of David, but all the while he was obedient to God, Saul, and his father, Jesse; David's kingdom was established forever because he had a pure heart toward the Lord, walked in his anointing, and waited patiently for God to bring his word to pass.

God, also established Christ's kingdom forever because his heart was pure; he fulfilled everything commanded him, prophesied of him, and was told by God, "Sit thou at my right hand, until I make thine enemies thy footstool." By righteousness, obedience, and patience, Christ, proved himself to be the Son of God and Son of David. Only the Messiah could prevail in this manner.

David wished to caution me and told me of the day when he went to bring up the ark of God. The ark of God was set upon a new cart and Uzzah put forth his hand upon the ark, because the oxen shook the cart and he thought to secure the ark. And the anger of the Lord was kindled against Uzzah; and God smote him there for his error; and there he died by the ark of God. This was surprising because the young man had lived with the ark in his father's house for years and had kept the commands concerning it, but this day thinking to show reverence openly towards it by touching the ark to secure it, he unknowingly broke the commandment and was punished for his disobedience. It was emphasized to me by David that the servants of God must serve him with all due seriousness and obey his every word to the letter; the best of intentions mean nothing to God against one of his commandments. We are not to do as we think it right to do, but we must obey God in all that we do. Obedience shows true reverence.

This lesson made David realize the importance of instructing his children; even at the moment of death he instructed Solomon. He spoke of innocent blood being charged against his house and looked to the day when the blood stain would be taken away. He also commanded Solomon to be strong, rule wisely, and keep the commandments of God. David guaranteed to his son, that if he was obedient and faithful that God would prosper all of his ways. God had promised David that he would establish his kingdom forever and said, "If thy children take heed to their way, to walk before me in truth with all their heart and with all their soul, there shall not fail thee (said he) a man on the throne of Israel." This alluded to the coming of Jesus.

Solomon had kept himself in all the ways of God: he was wiser than all men. As a youth Solomon wisely followed the instructions left by his father David, thus from an early age he followed in David's footsteps seeking to please God. He fulfilled David's desire of building a house for God to dwell in among the people. As God said to David, "Whereas it was in thine heart to build an house unto my name, thou didst well that it was in thine heart.

Nevertheless thou shalt not build the house; but thy son that shall come forth out of thy loins, he shall build the house unto my name." Solomon also acknowledged that God's house was built for the Jew and Gentile; he said, "Moreover concerning a stranger, that is not of thy people Israel, but cometh out of a far country for thy name's sake; (For they shall hear of thy great name, and of thy strong hand, and of thy stretched out arm;) when he shall come and pray toward this house; Hear thou in heaven thy dwelling place, and do according to all that the stranger calleth to thee for: that all people of the earth may know thy name, to fear thee, as do thy people Israel; and that they may know that this house, which I have builded, is called by thy name." Because Solomon honored God first and thought of the people before himself, God was pleased and gave him both what he asked for and blessed him with abundance. Solomon asked for wisdom, therefore God made him wiser than all men; he also received great riches and peace on all sides because it pleased God that he had David's heart.

God told Solomon, "I have heard thy prayer and thy supplication, that thou hast made before me: I have hallowed this house, which thou hast built, to put my name there for ever; and mine eyes and mine heart shall be there perpetually. And if thou wilt walk before me, as David thy father walked, in integrity of heart, and in uprightness, to do according to all that I have commanded thee, and wilt keep my statutes and my judgments: Then I will establish the throne of thy kingdom upon Israel for ever, as I promised to David thy father, saying, There shall not fail thee a man upon the throne of Israel." Because God had placed his name on an eternal temple, he had need of an eternal priest; God had also promised to established David's throne forever, Jesus fulfilled these promises because he was proven to be the eternal Priest and King.

Later in life Solomon left his first love and served other gods, but was shown favor by God for David's sake. God said, "Forasmuch as this is done of thee, and thou hast not kept my covenant and my statutes, which I have commanded thee, I will surely rend the kingdom from thee, and will give it to thy servant. Notwithstanding in thy days I will not do it for David thy father's sake: but I will rend it out of the hand of thy son. Howbeit I will not rend away all the kingdom; but will give one tribe to thy son for David my servant's sake, and for Jerusalem's sake which I have chosen." This reminded me of the favor shown Lott because of

Abraham. Solomon's testimony made me realize that all men in like manner have sinned but can be shown the favor of God, through the perfect blood of Jesus. For his sake we are forgiven.

Daniel had kept himself in all the ways of God: Daniel sat with Ezra, both taking their books, and with a pen divided the books up into chapters and verses for the purpose of easily relating the mystery to me. Daniel started with the decree to rebuild Jerusalem given by Artaxerxes in 457 B.C. (Ezra 7:13). He then said that God gave Israel 70 weeks (490 days), which he showed me to actually be 490 years. So from the time of the decree to rebuild Jerusalem, 490 years were given to Israel by God to end their rebellion and so the 490 year probation period would end 3.5 years after the death of Christ or (speaking to the future) 34 A.D. I heard in my spirit that forgiveness would be given (seventy times seven) to Israel as with a brother, which is 490. Three and a half years following Christ's death on the cross is when Israel ceased to be the sole people of God. I was shown in (Daniel 9:24-25) that the Messiah would be anointed 483 years (490-7) from the decree in 457 B.C. to rebuild Jerusalem(this being 27 A.D.) This being the exact year Jesus was baptized by John and was anointed by the Holy Spirit. "Messiah" means "Anointed One" and so this agrees with the time-line of the life of Jesus. Jesus appeared as the "Messiah" after 69 weeks and began his ministry on the 70th week (which is the last 7 years of the 490 year grace period). (Daniel 9:27) says, "And he shall confirm the covenant with many for one week: <u>and in the midst of the week he shall cause the sacrifice and the oblation to cease</u>, and for the overspreading of abominations he shall make it desolate, even until the consummation, and that determined shall be poured upon the desolate."

The term, "midst of the week", signifies <u>half of the 7 years</u> composing the final 70th week, <u>which is 3.5 years</u> which is the exact amount of time from the baptism of Jesus to his crucifixion (the length of his ministry). Jesus was crucified in 31 A.D. and, <u>the temple veil was rent from top to bottom, which ended of the</u>

sacrificial system. The sacrifices and oblations ceased at the death of Jesus because there is now no more need of them. Jesus is the only perfect sacrifice wholly acceptable to God. It is in the final 3.5 years of the 490 year grace period that the disciples were sent out to preach to and compel the Jews to be saved through Christ. In 34 A.D., the 70 weeks ended at the death of Stephen; Israel rejected the Gospel by stoning the messenger, the period of grace ended. Therefore, the Jews were no longer heirs to The Promise by birthright. The Gospel by default went to the Gentiles.

Ezra had kept himself in all the ways of God: he was a ready scribe. Artaxerxes, had sent Ezra to Jerusalem to deliver a freewill offering of himself and his counselors and to teach the commandments of God unto the people. He further wrote a decree which said, "And I, even I Artaxerxes the king, do make a decree to all the treasurers which are beyond the river, that whatsoever Ezra the priest, the scribe of the law of the God of heaven, shall require of you, it be done speedily, Unto an hundred talents of silver, and to an hundred measures of wheat, and to an hundred baths of wine, and to an hundred baths of oil, and salt without prescribing how much.

Whatsoever is commanded by the God of heaven, let it be diligently done for the house of the God of heaven: for why should there be wrath against the realm of the king and his sons? Also we certify you, that touching any of the priests and Levites, singers, porters, Nethinims, or ministers of this house of God, it shall not be lawful to impose toll, tribute, or custom, upon them." Because of the boldness which Ezra had spoken of God, he was ashamed to ask the king for soldiers to help guard the great sum of offerings en route to Jerusalem, even though the way was dangerous. Ezra said, "For I was ashamed to require of the king a band of soldiers and horsemen to help us against the enemy in the way: because we had spoken unto the king, saying, The hand of our God is upon all them for good that seek him; but his power and his wrath is against all them that forsake him." I saw this to be Godly shame and pride.

Artaxerxes had already pledged to give Ezra all that he required for his journey, but Ezra thought more highly of what was required by God of himself and all servants of God. Ezra, knew that God requires all of his children to walk by faith, by this unwavering faith, he honored the true king. Ezra, testified to Artaxerxes and his counselors about the mighty hand of God and wished not to mar his testimony by asking the help of man. Ezra also realized that the people had been slaves in Babylon because of sin and saw the decrees of the Persian Kings as a sign of God's favor returning to Israel. Once the favor of the true king had returned, there was no other need that required a man to fill it.

Ezra had waited on this decree to rebuild Jerusalem and understood the 70 week prophecy of Daniel, because of this, he looked to the coming of the Messiah, the True King. As a ready scribe, Ezra, was always ready to teach the commandments of God, but he knew from Israel's enslavement that man could not keep God's commands.

Captivity was his real world reminder of the consequences of sin. Ezra, looked to the coming of the Messiah to permanently remove sin away from the people. He looked for Jesus to free the people from the bondage of sin.

In paradise Ezra could clearly see that the people were still in bondage. He marked that the people still refused to sing the songs of Zion; how could they sing them in a strange land? He knew heaven to be his eternal home: this home is not a strange land, it is a land of eternal praise and rest. The Jews could not rest from sin, they could not sing the songs of Zion, because they were not in Zion. They were in Hell with the Gentiles.

Part IV: The Gentiles in Hell

The Lord handed me a cross, which due to the great weight of it, I felt to be made of iron; the weight of which was so great I could not hold it up with one hand even though it was of a proper size to be held in one hand. The Lord also placed his hand upon my heart, giving me the words that which to speak to the gentiles and as I began to speak his words they became a fire in my mouth. After this cleansing, I was commanded to cross the gulf and preach Christ crucified to the gentiles; at the invocation those who believe, accept, and confess Jesus as Lord & Savior are counted under the new covenant and taken up to heaven at the appointed time of Jesus. Most important of all I was told that this form of preaching, preaching to the dead, will never occur again; these were only given a chance to accept Christ because all men must be given this chance. After the resurrection a man who has heard Christ preached and dies without accepting Christ as Lord & Savior will be lost forever. After this word I was told that it was time for me to cross over to the other side.

There was a vast gulf fixed between paradise and the place of no hope. It would have taken me three days to cross it if there were a bridge, but I was caught-up by the wind and carried over to the other side; this only took about three hours. Satan followed me and gave secret command that the punishments should be increased that were inflicted upon the gentiles as I arrived; Satan followed shortly after me and ended all torments upon his arrival. As I began to preach Jesus, I became as Moses holding up the symbol of life in the wilderness, which is the cross of Christ; the agonies of all those that heard me was quieted while I spoke. Their torments had stopped but the gentiles had still been in agony from past torments. Jesus was the standard that was lifted up in this desert barren of hope, which all who accepted Jesus found hope and were relieved. On earth while above, Jesus became a curse, but in hell Christ became a cruse of water, thirstily shared. Jesus was the life-water offered the gentiles in this land of dead waters.

As I looked out into the endless masses of souls clustered together and restrained as if hanging from dead shrubs withered by the heat.

I remembered the words which David said, "But the sons of Belial shall be all of them as thorns thrust away, because they cannot be taken with hands." These souls were mostly white from the hellish environment surrounding them but each had a red blood stain upon them. They appeared to me as fields of cotton ready to be harvested but each was stained with blood as if workers had previously tried to harvest them but had pricked their hands on the bristles entangling them; there was an endless field of these. I almost said to myself that it was too much for one man to harvest alone in a day, but I remembered the words which Elijah spoke when he told me he once thought of himself as being left alone, but God revealed to him that He had reserved seven thousand workers for His purposes; I was made to realize that I was not alone the spirit of God was with me as well as two other witnesses, the Water and the Blood. I further remembered how Enoch walked with God, these thoughts rejuvenated me. I had to gird-up strength when I looked into the fields and saw the many droves of tormented souls swaying in the parched fusariumed air of hell.

I shook off the weaknesses and insecurities of my character, then I addressed the gentiles in hell and said, "Pardon me fathers of old, great kings of the earth, forgiveness my lords, because I know to some of you my manner of speech will be foreign, but I was commanded to speak to all times and in all tenses. Therefore I speak to you now and write unto others. But know this, the word of God has a specific meaning to every hearer, reader, and doer; to all that keep it. There is a word here for you today. My brothers it is important for you to know the truth, therefore I will relate it to you from the beginning of my message to the letter."

As I began to preach the relationship which exists between God, Jesus, and the Holy Spirit of God, I was greatly resisted by the children of antichrist which chanted, "Our God is one God, thou shalt love the Lord with all thy heart, mind, and soul; thou shalt have no other god before me." I asked these what is the second commandment and marveled because they gave me the third in place of the second. I preached to them that although there is a trinity, this harmony does not transgress the commandments nor does this revelation cause a man to transgress the law; Jesus Christ as part of the Godhead only fulfills God's desire to show his Son everything and elevate Jesus in the eyes of creation. I pleaded with them not to allow their flawed logic and misunderstandings of scripture to leave them where only faith in Jesus can pull them from. The Messiah is the word in the form of flesh which came down unto man to fulfill the holy scriptures. This is he that came by water and blood, even Jesus Christ; not by water only, but by water and blood. And it is the Spirit that beareth witness, because the Spirit is truth.

For there are three that bear record in heaven, the Father, the Word, and the Holy Ghost: and these three are one. And there are three that bear witness in earth, the spirit, and the water, and the blood: and these three agree in one. If we receive the witness of men, the witness of God is greater: for this is the witness of God which he hath testified of his Son. He that believeth on the Son of God hath the witness in himself: he that believeth not God hath made him a liar; because he believeth not the record that God gave of his Son. And this is the record, that God hath given to us eternal life, and this life is in his Son. He that hath the Son hath life; and he that hath not the Son of God hath not life.

As I began to preach the love of God in Christ Jesus I felt the spirit of the world which is antichrist and began to compel my brothers because the lusts of the world were still engrained within their hearts. "Love not the world, neither the things that are in the world. If any man love the world, the love of the Father is not in him. For all that is in the world, the lust of the flesh, and the lust of the eyes, and the pride of life, is not of the Father, but is of the world. And the world passeth away, and the lust thereof: but he that doeth the will of God abideth for ever. Little children, it is the last time: and as ye have heard that antichrist shall come, even now are there many antichrists; whereby we know that it is the last time. All that remain here shall be judged antichrist, but none that believe God and wait on the Lord will be ashamed. Whosoever denieth the Son, the same hath not the Father: he that acknowledgeth the Son hath the Father also. Let that therefore abide in you, which ye have heard from the beginning. If that which ye have heard from the beginning shall remain in you, ye also shall continue in the Son, and in the Father.

And this is the promise that he hath promised us, even eternal life. These things have I written unto you concerning them that seduce you. But the anointing which ye have received of him abideth in you, and ye need not that any man teach you: but as the same anointing teacheth you of all things, and is truth, and is no lie, and even as it hath taught you, ye shall abide in him. And now, little children, abide in him; that, when he shall appear, we may have confidence, and not be ashamed before him at his coming. If ye know that he is righteous, ye know that every one that doeth righteousness is born of him." The love of God through Christ Jesus was first shown to man when God sent his only son, Jesus, down to the earth in the form of flesh to die for the sins of the world.

As I began to preach the virgin birth, I was greatly resisted by some who insisted that the Messiah was to be born to a, "young girl", not a, "virgin". They claimed that through ignorance this idea of a "virgin birth" was upheld. For this cause they tried to bar-Jesus from being the Messiah. In fact it was, Barjesus; in fact, in hell there were 137 men who called themselves Barjesus. You should appreciate these facts because few escape hell, but there is an abundance of questions which await. I rebuked the powers and principalities, which tried to resist the testimony of Jesus. I continued to preach to the gentiles that there is nothing impossible for God and that man cannot dictate to God, how to be God. The terms, "young girl" and "virgin", both apply because Mary was both; this is God's doing and it only proves that man does not truly know the mind of God. I preached to them that if they accept the mind of Christ, they will realize that what seems impossible to men is but a small task for God. I told them that upon acceptance of Christ, the inner workings of things will be revealed to them because they are done to benefit them. Some further resisted the word and said that this idea of "virgin birth" came only after it was discovered that Jesus descended through his father, Joseph, who was descended from the cursed line of Jechoniah and therefore Jesus could not be king. I preached to these souls that Jesus descended from God the father in heaven and was adopted by Joseph after the miracle birth and thus became legal heir to the throne of David on his earthly father's side. Mary being descended of David through Solomon had already birthed Christ as a natural heir to the throne. Most important of all, Christ being descended from God made him complete heir to all of creation; the world and all that is within. A curse is a sign of sin, Jesus lived a life without sin, so we know and believe that there was no sin upon Jesus until the cross.

Jesus indeed took on sin when he became a curse for us, dying on the cross. Therefore, the only relevant sin of a distant ancestor is the sin that plagued all mankind; the sin of disobedience which was charged to Adam not the curse placed on Jechoniah. Jehovah God sent his only begotten son to remove Adam's sin and all sin from them that believe. Our God is a God of grace and he has proven this many times; I preached to them of the days of Noah and how God had repented of making man and swore to destroy mankind because of sin, yet Noah and his family was saved alive from the deluge. God ultimately repented from the total destruction he proposed to do unto mankind and he in like manner repented from the curse he placed on Jechoniah's heirs because Jechoniah changed his ways before God and was restored before his death. Through Jesus we were saved alive as Lot was saved alive through Abraham's favor with God.

These double-minded men on one hand held that God's word should be taken literally and not figuratively, but were found to be Hippocrates because they would not accept the testimony of Jesus preached by either means. They kept repeating that there is no room for man's interpretation of the word. I preached that there is no need of private interpretation but precept is built on precept;

through wisdom the saints in unity agree that God uses all avenues to speak to his children and his words contain truths for every generation, therefore by definition this is both literal and figurative. To show the literal and figurative I preached in their hearing the 70 week testimony of Daniel, but these men still refused to acknowledge Jesus as the Messiah. I then asked pharaoh if the children of Israel refused to follow Moses out of Egypt because he did not come to deliver them from sojourning in a strange land and bondage in Egypt at year 400 as it is written that God told Abraham? Did they argue to Moses that he nor anyone else could lead them from Egypt because 400 years had passed and that God's word had failed? Did God's word fail because Mary was a virgin or did the virgin birth help prove the power of God? The Torah affirms that 400 years were determined before deliverance of Israel out of Egypt, but God's timing said 430 years; was not this a foreshadowing of the coming of the Messiah? I saw Satan tremble at this word.

I preached that Jesus fulfilled the Torah as only the Messiah could. There were those that tried to withstand this word as Jannes and Jambres stood against Moses but the word I spoke was able more to heal than there divisive words could divide. In fact it was the uncircumcised unrepentant soul Korah, along with Jannes, and Jambres, which tried to withstand this word along with others. I saw many men of renown, many kings of old, and rich men who had died in their wickedness all looking at me attentively; these dead glares from blackened faces of stone alarmed me, but I heard Jesus say, "take no thought of their faces." This word comforted me and I could again see the white fields before me.

I continued to preach Jesus fulfilling the torah but was questioned by a rich man, Dives, who greatly resisted this word even after he saw me cross the chasm, from Abraham's bosom, and heard of how Jesus had conquered death itself and would show himself in Galilee to his brothers. Why would they not believe the word? Well Satan had convinced them that it was my master, Jesus, who had been causing their agony all these years because it was relieved only if they listened as I spoke the word of Jesus. Satan was so insidious for saying such a thing but I partly believed that there were some that did not hear because they could not hear the word of God. I preached that Jesus was a true prophet because he kept the Torah, spoke of the coming golden age, and as the Messiah he freed mankind from the punishments given to those which break the law.

Mankind has already proven that we cannot keep the law of God, therefore grace came down from above to cover us from sin.

Pharaoh demanded a sign but I had been given instruction not to give the gentiles a sign because the sign was already among them and they had everything there that was needed for belief and acceptance to occur. The word was spoken to each man, therefore each man had to decide for himself. As I looked into the endless crowds the finality of the situation hit me. This opportune moment was so special that it will never occur again. There were men standing upon one another, packed in to hear the word; even those who could not believe, did not want to leave this place.

There were those that held Ezra as the last prophet and upheld that Jesus could not be a prophet because the Jewish nation was still divided and many Jews were scattered throughout the world. They held that prophesy can only exist when the majority of Jews are gathered together under one nation. I preached to them that God does not need the Jewish nation to prophecy, it is Israel that needs God. Did not Balaam prophecy by God? Moses, himself wrote of Balaam as a prophet of God. These men would not hear, but only pointed to Balaam's gold as a way to discredit him. I told them that the testimony of Jesus Christ is prophecy, but they held firm to their incorrect belief that Jesus could not be the Messiah because he did not build a Jewish kingdom, did not build the temple of God, did not usher in universal peace, and did not spread the knowledge of God to the world. I preached that my presence with them was part of his plan of building an eternal kingdom with those who love the Lord.

The temple of God is not an earthly building to be destroyed, God's temple is spiritual and eternal. I preached even more passionately that the era of universal peace will occur at the second coming of Christ. And to counter their last claim I preached that not only will all the world be preached too and come to know the knowledge of God, but I was brought down to the underworld to preach Jesus and bring the knowledge of God to the forsaken, deaf, and blind. It is the word of God that Christ also hath once suffered for sins, the just for the unjust, that he might bring us to God, being put to death in the flesh, but quickened by the Spirit: By which also he went and preached unto the spirits in prison.

I preached Christ crucified for the sins of the world and some wanted proof and wondered why Jesus did not come himself to speak with them. They wondered at this preaching that was done in their hearing and could not receive anything I said on the basis of faith.

Some held that every age has a "messiah" because the word means, "anointed of God". There was one there who held that he was once the messiah and that his throne was taken away from him. I saw this to be the same "virgin birth" argument again and repeated to the souls that the entirety of God's ways are not known to man, neither can we counsel God on which paths to take or choices to make. That is why also it is contained in the scripture, Behold, I lay in Sion a chief corner stone, elect, precious: and he that believeth on him shall not be confounded. Unto you therefore which believe he is precious: but unto them which be disobedient, the stone which the builders disallowed, the same is made the head of the corner, And a stone of stumbling, and a rock of offence, even to them which stumble at the word, being disobedient: whereunto also they were appointed. The elect of God can never be lost, but ye are a chosen generation, a royal priesthood, an holy nation, a peculiar people; that ye should shew forth the praises of him who hath called you out of darkness into his marvelous light: Which in time past were not a people, but are now the people of God: which had not obtained mercy, but now have obtained mercy. At the end of these sayings and preachings I asked the souls to accept Jesus as Lord and Savior and to repent from their past sins. And when the Gentiles heard this, they were glad, and glorified the word of the Lord: and as many as were ordained to eternal life believed. I asked all these to stand with me.

At this saying Satan began to speak, still pretending to be God, and ends the agonies of the gentiles completely. He tells them that they have been purged of all sin through punishment and can now follow him across the gulf into paradise. He also uses my own words against me and reminds the gentiles that I said, "All that remain here shall be judged antichrist, but none that believe God and wait on the Lord will be ashamed." It is then I noticed that Satan has given himself the guise and similitude of Moses to present a false glory.

Many believe Satan and follow him into the air to cross the gulf but it is so wide that it will take three days to cross using the bridge made of water, which Satan generated. Let me be clear, Satan, generated the bridge, not the water. The gentiles began to cross over by city, because that's how the Counsel of Four kept them divided to prepare for the judgment. I began to plead with those who crossed over into the air to keep them from following Satan, but many struck me as I tried to pull them away from the abyss. Each man that passed over wounded me with a painful blow; whether by hand or not I cannot tell, but it pained me completely to see so many lost. As almost every soul in hell follows Satan out onto the liquid bridge, I fell to the ground as dead at the sight of the impending tragedy. Satan takes them out far enough into the gulf and then pulls away the bridge from beneath them! *The lost souls all fall down into the lower parts of Hell!*

As I turned away from the most horrific scene, I trembled and quaked in agony. The terrors of hell compassed me about and pierced my very soul; I felt as if my spirit itself began to lose strength and bleed out. But then, I glimpsed and sighted upon the few precious souls which in the middle of Sheol were spared because they heard and believed the voice of God. Not my voice but that of their Creator and Redeemer. My spirit was healed when I looked upon those few treasured pure white souls and I glorified God in a manner of hymn and song that would have put David to shame and these glorified with me. Even in the depths of hell with tears and heartache abounding, I found a reason to praise God. It was then in the midst of praise that I saw the temple of God. I saw it in these few tortured and tried souls which had converted from evil practices and took on the garment of faith in Christ Jesus; he had made me glad.

The red blood stain was no longer on these souls, which had been washed in the blood of the lamb. This temple not made by human hands was beautiful in its own right. The first city of Hell was to be abandoned forever, which made these singular souls all the more valuable in my sight, but in the eyes of God they have always maintained this value. They have always been precious.

These things I write unto you that you may know for yourselves the mystery of the Lord, which brings joy. Jesus walked the true path as only he could because only he remained true to the commandments given him by God. Christ fulfilled all that was prophesied of him and on the third day rose from the grave with all power and glory given to him of the father in heaven and earth. Because he was given a name above every name, neither death nor hell could hold him. Let praise, glory, and majesty be to God forever through Christ Jesus our Lord, Amen.

Part V: The Resurrection

Matthew 28:1-10

1. In the end of the sabbath, as it began to dawn toward the first day of the week, came Mary Magdalene and the other Mary to see the sepulchre.

2. And, behold, there was a great earthquake: for the angel of the Lord descended from heaven, and came and rolled back the stone from the door, and sat upon it.

3. His countenance was like lightning, and his raiment white as snow:

4. And for fear of him the keepers did shake, and became as dead men.

5. And the angel answered and said unto the women, Fear not ye: for I know that ye seek Jesus, which was crucified.

6. He is not here: for he is risen, as he said. Come, see the place where the Lord lay.

7. And go quickly, and tell his disciples that he is risen from the dead; and, behold, he goeth before you into Galilee; there shall ye see him: lo, I have told you.

8. And they departed quickly from the sepulchre with fear and great joy; and did run to bring his disciples word.

9. And as they went to tell his disciples, behold, Jesus met them, saying, All hail. And they came and held him by the feet, and worshipped him.

10. Then said Jesus unto them, Be not afraid: go tell my brethren that they go into Galilee, and there shall they see me.

Bible Verses:

<u>John 5:1-47</u>

After this there was a feast of the Jews; and Jesus went up to Jerusalem. Now there is at Jerusalem by the sheep market a pool, which is called in the Hebrew tongue Bethesda, having five porches. In these lay a great multitude of impotent folk, of blind, halt, withered, waiting for the moving of the water. For an angel went down at a certain season into the pool, and troubled the water: whosoever then first after the troubling of the water stepped in was made whole of whatsoever disease he had. And a certain man was there, which had an infirmity thirty and eight years. When Jesus saw him lie, and knew that he had been now a long time in that case, he saith unto him, Wilt thou be made whole? The impotent man answered him, Sir, I have no man, when the water is troubled, to put me into the pool: but while I am coming, another steppeth down before me. Jesus saith unto him, Rise, take up thy bed, and walk. And immediately the man was made whole, and took up his bed, and walked: and on the same day was the sabbath. The Jews therefore said unto him that was cured, It is the sabbath day: it is not lawful for thee to carry thy bed.

He answered them, He that made me whole, the same said unto me, Take up thy bed, and walk. Then asked they him, What man is that which said unto thee, Take up thy bed, and walk? And he that was healed wist not who it was: for Jesus had conveyed himself away, a multitude being in that place. Afterward Jesus findeth him in the temple, and said unto him, Behold, thou art made whole: sin no more, lest a worse thing come unto thee. The man departed, and told the Jews that it was Jesus, which had made him whole. And therefore did the Jews persecute Jesus, and sought to slay him, because he had done these things on the sabbath day. But Jesus answered them, My Father worketh hitherto, and I work. Therefore the Jews sought the more to kill him, because he not only had broken the sabbath, but said also that God was his Father, making himself equal with God. Then answered Jesus and said unto them, Verily, verily, I say unto you, The Son can do nothing of himself, but what he seeth the Father do: for what things soever he doeth, these also doeth the Son likewise. For the Father loveth the Son, and sheweth him all things that himself doeth: and he will shew him greater works than these, that ye may marvel. For as the Father raiseth up the dead, and quickeneth them; even so the Son quickeneth whom he will. For the Father judgeth no man, but hath committed all judgment unto the Son: That all men should honour the Son, even as they honour the Father. He that honoureth not the Son honoureth not the Father which hath sent him. Verily, verily, I say unto you, He that heareth my word, and believeth on him that sent me, hath everlasting life, and shall not come into condemnation; but is passed from death unto life. Verily, verily, I say unto you, The hour is coming, and now is, when the dead shall hear the voice of the Son of God: and they that hear shall live. For as the Father hath life in himself; so hath he given to the Son to have life in himself; And hath given him authority to execute judgment also, because he is the Son of man. Marvel not at this: for the hour is coming, in the which all that are in the graves shall hear his voice, And shall come forth; they that have done good, unto the resurrection of life; and they that have done evil, unto the resurrection of damnation. I can of mine own self do nothing: as I hear, I judge: and my judgment is just; because I seek not mine own will, but the will of the Father which hath sent me. If I bear witness of myself, my witness is not true.

There is another that beareth witness of me; and I know that the witness which he witnesseth of me is true. Ye sent unto John, and he bare witness unto the truth. But I receive not testimony from man: but these things I say, that ye might be saved. He was a burning and a shining light: and ye were willing for a season to rejoice in his light. But I have greater witness than that of John: for the works which the Father hath given me to finish, the same works that I do, bear witness of me, that the Father hath sent me. And the Father himself, which hath sent me, hath borne witness of me. Ye have neither heard his voice at any time, nor seen his shape. And ye have not his word abiding in you: for whom he hath sent, him ye believe not.

Search the scriptures; for in them ye think ye have eternal life: and they are they which testify of me. And ye will not come to me, that ye might have life. I receive not honour from men. But I know you, that ye have not the love of God in you. I am come in my Father's name, and ye receive me not: if another shall come in his own name, him ye will receive. How can ye believe, which receive honour one of another, and seek not the honour that cometh from God only? Do not think that I will accuse you to the Father: there is one that accuseth you, even Moses, in whom ye trust. For had ye believed Moses, ye would have believed me: for he wrote of me. But if ye believe not his writings, how shall ye believe my words?

Mark 11:15-18

And they come to Jerusalem: and Jesus went into the temple, and began to cast out them that sold and bought in the temple, and overthrew the tables of the moneychangers, and the seats of them that sold doves; And would not suffer that any man should carry any vessel through the temple. And he taught, saying unto them, Is it not written, My house shall be called of all nations the house of prayer? but ye have made it a den of thieves. And the scribes and chief priests heard it, and sought how they might destroy him: for they feared him, because all the people was astonished at his doctrine.

Matthew 21:15-16

And the blind and the lame came to him in the temple; and he healed them. And when the chief priests and scribes saw the wonderful things that he did, and the children crying in the temple, and saying, Hosanna to the Son of David; they were sore displeased. And said unto him, Hearest thou what these say? And Jesus saith unto them, Yea; have ye never read, Out of the mouth of babes and sucklings thou hast perfected praise?

Matthew 21:23-32

And when he was come into the temple, the chief priests and the elders of the people came unto him as he was teaching, and said, By what authority doest thou these things? and who gave thee this authority? And Jesus answered and said unto them, I also will ask you one thing, which if ye tell me, I in like wise will tell you by what authority I do these things. The baptism of John, whence was it? from heaven, or of men? And they reasoned with themselves, saying, If we shall say, From heaven; he will say unto us, Why did ye not then believe him? But if we shall say, Of men; we fear the people; for all hold John as a prophet. And they answered Jesus, and said, We cannot tell. And he said unto them, Neither tell I you by what authority I do these things. But what think ye? A certain man had two sons; and he came to the first, and said, Son, go work to day in my vineyard. He answered and said, I will not: but afterward he repented, and went. And he came to the second, and said likewise. And he answered and said, I go, sir: and went not. Whether of them twain did the will of his father? They say unto him, The first. Jesus saith unto them, Verily I say unto you, That the publicans and the harlots go into the kingdom of God before you. For John came unto you in the way of righteousness, and ye believed him not: but the publicans and the harlots believed him: and ye, when ye had seen it, repented not afterward, that ye might believe him.

Luke 6:1-5

And it came to pass on the second sabbath after the first, that he went through the corn fields; and his disciples plucked the ears of corn, and did eat, rubbing them in their hands. And certain of the Pharisees said unto them, Why do ye that which is not lawful to do on the sabbath days? And Jesus answering them said, Have ye not read so much as this, what David did, when himself was an hungred, and they which were with him; How he went into the house of God, and did take and eat the shewbread, and gave also to them that were with him; which it is not lawful to eat but for the priests alone?

And he said unto them, That the Son of man is Lord also of the sabbath.

John 10:16-18

And other sheep I have, which are not of this fold: them also I must bring, and they shall hear my voice; and there shall be one fold, and one shepherd. Therefore doth my Father love me, because I lay down my life, that I might take it again. No man taketh it from me, but I lay it down of myself. I have power to lay it down, and I have power to take it again. This commandment have I received of my Father.

John 11:47-48

What are we accomplishing?" they asked. "Here is this man performing many miraculous signs. If we let him go on like this, everyone will believe in him, and then the Romans will come and take away both our place and our nation."

Matthew 26:71-75

And when he was gone out into the porch, another maid saw him, and said unto them that were there, This fellow was also with Jesus of Nazareth. And again he denied with an oath, I do not know the man. And after a while came unto him they that stood by, and said to Peter, Surely thou also art one of them; for thy speech bewrayeth thee. Then began he to curse and to swear, saying, I know not the man. And immediately the cock crew. And Peter remembered the word of Jesus, which said unto him, Before the cock crow, thou shalt deny me thrice. And he went out, and wept bitterly.

Zechariah 13:7-9

Awake, O sword, against my shepherd, and against the man that is my fellow, saith the LORD of hosts: smite the shepherd, and the sheep shall be scattered: and I will turn mine hand upon the little ones. And it shall come to pass, that in all the land, saith the LORD, two parts therein shall be cut off and die; but the third shall be left therein. And I will bring the third part through the fire, and will refine them as silver is refined, and will try them as gold is tried: they shall call on my name, and I will hear them: I will say, It is my people: and they shall say, The LORD is my God.

Isaiah 53:5

But he was wounded for our transgressions, he was bruised for our iniquities: the chastisement of our peace was upon him; and with his stripes we are healed.

Luke 23:33

And when they were come to the place, which is called Calvary, there they crucified him, and the malefactors, one on the right hand, and the other on the left.

Job 38:17

Have the gates of death been opened unto thee? or hast thou seen the doors of the shadow of death?

Luke 23:34

Then said Jesus, Father, forgive them; for they know not what they do. And they parted his raiment, and cast lots.

Luke 23:43

And Jesus said unto him, Verily I say unto thee, To day shalt thou be with me in paradise.

John 19:25-27

Now there stood by the cross of Jesus his mother, and his mother's sister, Mary the wife of Cleophas, and Mary Magdalene. When Jesus therefore saw his mother, and the disciple standing by, whom he loved, he saith unto his mother, Woman, behold thy son! Then saith he to the disciple, Behold thy mother! And from that hour that disciple took her unto his own home.

Mark 15:34

And at the ninth hour Jesus cried with a loud voice, saying, Eloi, Eloi, lama sabachthani? which is, being interpreted, My God, my God, why hast thou forsaken me?

Psalm 22:1

My God, my God, why hast thou forsaken me? why art thou so far from helping me, and from the words of my roaring?

John 19:28

After this, Jesus knowing that all things were now accomplished, that the scripture might be fulfilled, saith, I thirst.

John 19:30

When Jesus therefore had received the vinegar, he said, It is finished: and he bowed his head, and gave up the ghost.

Luke 23:46

And when Jesus had cried with a loud voice, he said, Father, into thy hands I commend my spirit: and having said thus, he gave up the ghost.

Luke 23:34-49

Then said Jesus, Father, forgive them; for they know not what they do. And they parted his raiment, and cast lots. And the people stood beholding. And the rulers also with them derided him, saying, He saved others; let him save himself, if he be Christ, the chosen of God. And the soldiers also mocked him, coming to him, and offering him vinegar, And saying, If thou be the king of the Jews, save thyself. And a superscription also was written over him in letters of Greek, and Latin, and Hebrew, THIS IS THE KING OF THE JEWS. And one of the malefactors which were hanged railed on him, saying, If thou be Christ, save thyself and us. But the other answering rebuked him, saying, Dost not thou fear God, seeing thou art in the same condemnation? And we indeed justly; for we receive the due reward of our deeds: but this man hath done nothing amiss. And he said unto Jesus, Lord, remember me when thou comest into thy kingdom. And Jesus said unto him, Verily I say unto thee, Today shalt thou be with me in paradise. And it was about the sixth hour, and there was a darkness over all the earth until the ninth hour. And the sun was darkened, and the veil of the temple was rent in the midst. And when Jesus had cried with a loud voice, he said, Father, into thy hands I commend my spirit: and having said thus, he gave up the ghost. Now when the centurion saw what was done, he glorified God, saying, Certainly this was a righteous man. And all the people that came together to that sight, beholding the things which were done, smote their breasts, and returned. And all his acquaintance, and the women that followed him from Galilee, stood afar off, beholding these things.

John 19:29-30

Now there was set a vessel full of vinegar: and they filled a spunge with vinegar, and put it upon hyssop, and put it to his mouth. When

Jesus therefore had received the vinegar, he said, It is finished: and he bowed his head, and gave up the ghost.

John 19:34

But one of the soldiers with a spear pierced his side, and forthwith came there out blood and water.

I Timothy 2:14-15

And Adam was not deceived, but the woman being deceived was in the transgression. Notwithstanding she shall be saved in childbearing, if they continue in faith and charity and holiness with sobriety.

Hebrews 4:12

For the word of God is quick, and powerful, and sharper than any twoedged sword, piercing even to the dividing asunder of soul and spirit, and of the joints and marrow, and is a discerner of the thoughts and intents of the heart.

Genesis 6:3

And the LORD said, My spirit shall not always strive with man, for that he also is flesh: yet his days shall be an hundred and twenty years.

Collosians 2:13-16

And you, being dead in your sins and the uncircumcision of your flesh, hath he quickened together with him, having forgiven you all trespasses; Blotting out the handwriting of ordinances that was against us, which was contrary to us, and took it out of the way, nailing it to his cross; And having spoiled principalities and powers, he made a shew of them openly , triumphing over them in it. Let no man therefore judge you in meat, or in drink, or in respect of an holyday, or of the new moon, or of the sabbath days:

1 Corinthians 15:45

And so it is written. The first Adam was made a living soul; the last Adam was made a quickening spirit.

Revelations 17:14

These shall make war with the Lamb, and the Lamb shall overcome them: for he is Lord of lords, and King of kings: and they that are with him are called, and chosen, and faithful.

John 16:8-11

And when he is come, he will reprove the world of sin, and of righteousness, and of judgment:

Of sin, because they believe not on me; Of righteousness, because I go to my Father, and ye see me no more; Of judgment, because the prince of this world is judged.

John 12:31-32

Now is the judgment of this world: now shall the prince of this world be cast out. And I, if I be lifted up from the earth, will draw all men unto me.

Romans 5:12-21

Wherefore, as by one man sin entered into the world, and death by sin; and so death passed upon all men, for that all have sinned: (For until the law sin was in the world: but sin is not imputed when there is no law. Nevertheless death reigned from Adam to Moses, even over them that had not sinned after the similitude of Adam's transgression, who is the figure of him that was to come. But not as the offence, so also is the free gift. For if through the offence of one many be dead, much more the grace of God, and the gift by grace, which is by one man, Jesus Christ, hath abounded unto many. And not as it was by one that sinned, so is the gift: for the judgment was by one to condemnation, but the free gift is of many offences unto justification. For if by one man's offence death reigned by one; much more they which receive abundance of grace and of the gift of righteousness shall reign in life by one, Jesus Christ.) Therefore as by the offence of one judgment came upon all men to condemnation; even so by the righteousness of one the free gift came upon all men unto justification of life. For as by one man's disobedience many were made sinners, so by the obedience of one shall many be made righteous. Moreover the law entered, that the offence might abound. But where sin abounded, grace did much more abound: That as sin hath reigned unto death, even so might grace reign through righteousness unto eternal life by Jesus Christ our Lord.

2 Samuel 23:6

But the sons of Belial shall be all of them as thorns thrust away, because they cannot be taken with hands:

1 Kings 2:4

That the LORD may continue his word which he spake concerning me, saying, If thy children take heed to their way, to walk before me in truth with all their heart and with all their soul, there shall not fail thee (said he) a man on the throne of Israel.

1 Corinthians 1:20-25

Where is the wise? where is the scribe? where is the disputer of this world? hath not God made foolish the wisdom of this world? For after that in the wisdom of God the world by wisdom knew not

God, it pleased God by the foolishness of preaching to save them that believe. For the Jews require a sign, and the Greeks seek after wisdom: But we preach Christ crucified, unto the Jews a stumblingblock, and unto the Greeks foolishness; But unto them which are called, both Jews and Greeks, Christ the power of God, and the wisdom of God. Because the foolishness of God is wiser than men; and the weakness of God is stronger than men.

1 John 4:7-11

Beloved, let us love one another: for love is of God; and every one that loveth is born of God, and knoweth God. He that loveth not knoweth not God; for God is love. In this was manifested the love of God toward us, because that God sent his only begotten Son into the world, that we might live through him. Herein is love, not that we loved God, but that he loved us, and sent his Son to be the propitiation for our sins. Beloved, if God so loved us, we ought also to love one another.

Romans 10:13-15

For whosoever shall call upon the name of the Lord shall be saved. How then shall they call on him in whom they have not believed? and how shall they believe in him of whom they have not heard? and how shall they hear without a preacher? And how shall they preach, except they be sent? as it is written, How beautiful are the feet of them that preach the gospel of peace, and bring glad tidings of good things!

Ephesians 1:9-14

Having made known unto us the mystery of his will, according to his good pleasure which he hath purposed in himself: That in the dispensation of the fulness of times he might gather together in one all things in Christ, both which are in heaven, and which are on earth; even in him: In whom also we have obtained an inheritance, being predestinated according to the purpose of him who worketh all things after the counsel of his own will: That we should be to the praise of his glory, who first trusted in Christ. In whom ye also trusted, after that ye heard the word of truth, the gospel of your salvation: in whom also after that ye believed, ye were sealed with that holy Spirit of promise, Which is the earnest of our inheritance until the redemption of the purchased possession, unto the praise of his glory.

Genesis 45:5-8

Now therefore be not grieved, nor angry with yourselves, that ye sold me hither: for God did send me before you to preserve life. For these two years hath the famine been in the land: and yet there are five years, in the which there shall neither be earing nor harvest. And God sent me before you to preserve you a posterity in the earth, and to save your lives by a great deliverance. So now it was not you that sent me hither, but God: and he hath made me a father to Pharaoh, and lord of all his house, and a ruler throughout all the land of Egypt.

Deuteronomy 31:19-22

Now therefore write ye this song for you, and teach it the children of Israel: put it in their mouths, that this song may be a witness for me against the children of Israel. For when I shall have brought them into the land which I sware unto their fathers, that floweth with milk and honey; and they shall have eaten and filled themselves, and waxen fat; then will they turn unto other gods, and serve them, and provoke me, and break my covenant. And it shall come to pass, when many evils and troubles are befallen them, that this song shall testify against them as a witness; for it shall not be forgotten out of the mouths of their seed: for I know their imagination which they go about, even now, before I have brought them into the land which I sware. Moses therefore wrote this song the same day, and taught it the children of Israel.

Hebrews 12:1-2

Wherefore seeing we also are compassed about with so great a cloud of witnesses, let us lay aside every weight, and the sin which doth so easily beset us, and let us run with patience the race that is set before us, Looking unto Jesus the author and finisher of our faith; who for the joy that was set before him endured the cross, despising the shame, and is set down at the right hand of the throne of God.

Exodus 24:7-8

And he took the book of the covenant, and read in the audience of the people: and they said, All that the LORD hath said will we do, and be obedient. And Moses took the blood, and sprinkled it on the people, and said, Behold the blood of the covenant, which the LORD hath made with you concerning all these words.

I John 4:18

There is no fear in love; but perfect love casteth out fear: because fear hath torment. He that feareth is not made perfect in love.

Matthew 8:26-27

And he saith unto them, Why are ye fearful, O ye of little faith? Then he arose, and rebuked the winds and the sea; and there was a great calm. 27But the men marvelled, saying, What manner of man is this, that even the winds and the sea obey him!

Job 1:21-22

And said, Naked came I out of my mother's womb, and naked shall I return thither: the LORD gave, and the LORD hath taken away; blessed be the name of the LORD. In all this Job sinned not, nor charged God foolishly.

Job 2:9-10

Then said his wife unto him, Dost thou still retain thine integrity? curse God, and die. But he said unto her, Thou speakest as one of the foolish women speaketh. What? shall we receive good at the hand of God, and shall we not receive evil? In all this did not Job sin with his lips.

Job 6:4

For the arrows of the Almighty are within me, the poison whereof drinketh up my spirit: the terrors of God do set themselves in array against me.

Job 13:15

Though he slay me, yet will I trust in him: but I will maintain mine own ways before him.

Matthew 19:29

And every one that hath forsaken houses, or brethren, or sisters, or father, or mother, or wife, or children, or lands, for my name's sake, shall receive an hundredfold, and shall inherit everlasting life.

Job 14:14

If a man die, shall he live again? all the days of my appointed time will I wait, till my change come.

Job 19:25-26

For I know that my redeemer liveth, and that he shall stand at the latter day upon the earth: And though after my skin worms destroy this body, yet in my flesh shall I see God:

Job 16:19

Also now, behold, my witness is in heaven, and my record is on high.

Job 42:12-13

So the LORD blessed the latter end of Job more than his beginning: for he had fourteen thousand sheep, and six thousand camels, and a thousand yoke of oxen, and a thousand she asses. He had also seven sons and three daughters.

I Samuel 2:1-3

And Hannah prayed, and said, My heart rejoiceth in the LORD, mine horn is exalted in the LORD: my mouth is enlarged over mine enemies; because I rejoice in thy salvation. There is none holy as the LORD: for there is none beside thee: neither is there any rock like our God. Talk no more so exceeding proudly; let not arrogancy come out of your mouth: for the LORD is a God of knowledge, and by him actions are weighed. I Samuel 2:9-10

He will keep the feet of his saints, and the wicked shall be silent in darkness; for by strength shall no man prevail. The adversaries of the LORD shall be broken to pieces; out of heaven shall he thunder upon them: the LORD shall judge the ends of the earth; and he shall give strength unto his king, and exalt the horn of his anointed.

I Samuel 3:18

And Samuel told him every whit, and hid nothing from him. And he said, It is the LORD: let him do what seemeth him good.

I Samuel 2:30

Wherefore the LORD God of Israel saith, I said indeed that thy house, and the house of thy father, should walk before me for ever:

but now the LORD saith, Be it far from me; for them that honour me I will honour, and they that despise me shall be lightly esteemed.

Matthew 17:1-5

And after six days Jesus taketh Peter, James, and John his brother, and bringeth them up into an high mountain apart, And was transfigured before them: and his face did shine as the sun, and his raiment was white as the light. And, behold, there appeared unto them Moses and Elias talking with him. Then answered Peter, and said unto Jesus, Lord, it is good for us to be here: if thou wilt, let us make here three tabernacles; one for thee, and one for Moses, and one for Elias. While he yet spake, behold, a bright cloud overshadowed them: and behold a voice out of the cloud, which said, This is my beloved Son, in whom I am well pleased; hear ye him.

John 5:30

I can of mine own self do nothing: as I hear, I judge: and my judgment is just; because I seek not mine own will, but the will of the Father which hath sent me.

Hebrews 9:13-14

For if the blood of bulls and of goats, and the ashes of an heifer sprinkling the unclean, sanctifieth to the purifying of the flesh: How much more shall the blood of Christ, who through the eternal Spirit offered himself without spot to God, purge your conscience from dead works to serve the living God?

Hebrews 9:22

And almost all things are by the law purged with blood; and without shedding of blood is no remission.

1 Samuel 15:17-26

And Samuel said, When thou wast little in thine own sight, wast thou not made the head of the tribes of Israel, and the LORD anointed thee king over Israel? And the LORD sent thee on a journey, and said, Go and utterly destroy the sinners the Amalekites, and fight against them until they be consumed. Wherefore then didst thou not obey the voice of the LORD, but didst fly upon the spoil, and didst evil in the sight of the LORD? And Saul said unto Samuel, Yea, I have obeyed the voice of the LORD, and have gone the way which the LORD sent me, and have brought Agag the king of Amalek, and have utterly destroyed the Amalekites. But the people took of the spoil, sheep and oxen, the chief of the things which should have been utterly destroyed, to sacrifice unto the LORD thy God in Gilgal. And Samuel said, Hath the LORD as great delight in burnt offerings and sacrifices, as in obeying the voice of the LORD? Behold, to obey is better than sacrifice, and to hearken than the fat of rams. For rebellion is as the sin of witchcraft, and stubbornness is as iniquity and idolatry. Because thou hast rejected the word of the LORD, he hath also rejected thee from being king. And Saul said unto Samuel, I have sinned: for I have transgressed the commandment of the LORD, and thy words: because I feared the people, and obeyed their voice. Now therefore, I pray thee, pardon my sin, and turn again with me, that I may worship the LORD. And Samuel said unto Saul, I will not return with thee: for thou hast rejected the word of the LORD, and the LORD hath rejected thee from being king over Israel.

Daniel 9:27

And he shall confirm the covenant with many for one week: and in the midst of the week he shall cause the sacrifice and the oblation to cease, and for the overspreading of abominations he shall make it desolate, even until the consummation, and that determined shall be poured upon the desolate.

Matthew 18:21-22

Then came Peter to him, and said, Lord, how oft shall my brother sin against me, and I forgive him? till seven times? Jesus saith unto him, I say not unto thee, Until seven times: but, Until seventy times seven.

Revelations 12:10-11

And I heard a loud voice saying in heaven, Now is come salvation, and strength, and the kingdom of our God, and the power of his Christ: for the accuser of our brethren is cast down, which accused them before our God day and night. And they overcame him by the blood of the Lamb, and by the word of their testimony; and they loved not their lives unto the death.

1 John 5:5-12

Who is he that overcometh the world, but he that believeth that Jesus is the Son of God? This is he that came by water and blood, even Jesus Christ; not by water only, but by water and blood. And it is the Spirit that beareth witness, because the Spirit is truth. For there are three that bear record in heaven, the Father, the Word, and the Holy Ghost: and these three are one. And there are three that bear witness in earth, the spirit, and the water, and the blood: and these three agree in one. If we receive the witness of men, the witness of God is greater: for this is the witness of God which he hath testified of his Son. He that believeth on the Son of God hath the witness in himself: he that believeth not God hath made him a liar; because he believeth not the record that God gave of his Son.

And this is the record, that God hath given to us eternal life, and this life is in his Son. He that hath the Son hath life; and he that hath not the Son of God hath not life.

Psalms 25:2-3

O my God, I trust in thee: let me not be ashamed, let not mine enemies triumph over me. Yea, let none that wait on thee be ashamed: let them be ashamed which transgress without cause.

I Samuel 26:23-25

The LORD render to every man his righteousness and his faithfulness: for the LORD delivered thee into my hand to day, but I would not stretch forth mine hand against the LORD'S anointed.

And, behold, as thy life was much set by this day in mine eyes, so let my life be much set by in the eyes of the LORD, and let him deliver me out of all tribulation. Then Saul said to David, Blessed be thou, my son David: thou shalt both do great things, and also shalt still prevail. So David went on his way, and Saul returned to his place.

Psalms 110:1

The LORD said unto my Lord, Sit thou at my right hand, until I make thine enemies thy footstool.

2 Samuel 6:1-11

Again, David gathered together all the chosen men of Israel, thirty thousand. And David arose, and went with all the people that were with him from Baale of Judah, to bring up from thence the ark of God, whose name is called by the name of the LORD of hosts that dwelleth between the cherubims. And they set the ark of God upon a new cart, and brought it out of the house of Abinadab that was in Gibeah: and Uzzah and Ahio, the sons of Abinadab, drave the new cart. And they brought it out of the house of Abinadab which was at Gibeah, accompanying the ark of God: and Ahio went before the ark. And David and all the house of Israel played before the LORD on all manner of instruments made of fir wood, even on harps, and on psalteries, and on timbrels, and on cornets, and on cymbals. And when they came to Nachon's threshingfloor, Uzzah put forth his hand to the ark of God, and took hold of it; for the oxen shook it. And the anger of the LORD was kindled against Uzzah; and God smote him there for his error; and there he died by the ark of God. And David was displeased, because the LORD had made a breach upon Uzzah: and he called the name of the place Perezuzzah to this day. And David was afraid of the LORD that day, and said, How shall the ark of the LORD come to me? So David would not remove the ark of the LORD unto him into the city of David: but David carried it aside into the house of Obededom the Gittite. And the ark of the LORD continued in the house of Obededom the Gittite three months: and the LORD blessed Obededom, and all his household.

1 Kings 8:18-19

And the LORD said unto David my father, Whereas it was in thine heart to build an house unto my name, thou didst well that it was in thine heart. Nevertheless thou shalt not build the house; but thy son that shall come forth out of thy loins, he shall build the house unto my name.

1 Kings 8:41-43

Moreover concerning a stranger, that is not of thy people Israel, but cometh out of a far country for thy name's sake; (For they shall hear of thy great name, and of thy strong hand, and of thy stretched out arm;) when he shall come and pray toward this house; Hear thou in heaven thy dwelling place, and do according to all that the stranger calleth to thee for: that all people of the earth may know thy name, to fear thee, as do thy people Israel; and that they may know that this house, which I have builded, is called by thy name.

1 Kings 9:3-5

And the LORD said unto him, I have heard thy prayer and thy supplication, that thou hast made before me: I have hallowed this house, which thou hast built, to put my name there for ever; and mine eyes and mine heart shall be there perpetually. And if thou wilt walk before me, as David thy father walked, in integrity of heart, and in uprightness, to do according to all that I have commanded thee, and wilt keep my statutes and my judgments: Then I will establish the throne of thy kingdom upon Israel for ever, as I promised to David thy father, saying, There shall not fail thee a man upon the throne of Israel.

1 Kings 11:11-13

Wherefore the LORD said unto Solomon, Forasmuch as this is done of thee, and thou hast not kept my covenant and my statutes, which I have commanded thee, I will surely rend the kingdom from thee, and will give it to thy servant. Notwithstanding in thy days I will not do it for David thy father's sake: but I will rend it out of the hand of thy son. Howbeit I will not rend away all the kingdom; but will give one tribe to thy son for David my servant's sake, and for Jerusalem's sake which I have chosen.

Ezra 7:21-24

And I, even I Artaxerxes the king, do make a decree to all the treasurers which are beyond the river, that whatsoever Ezra the priest, the scribe of the law of the God of heaven, shall require of you, it be done speedily, Unto an hundred talents of silver, and to an hundred measures of wheat, and to an hundred baths of wine, and to an hundred baths of oil, and salt without prescribing how much.

Whatsoever is commanded by the God of heaven, let it be diligently done for the house of the God of heaven: for why should there be wrath against the realm of the king and his sons? Also we certify you, that touching any of the priests and Levites, singers, porters, Nethinims, or ministers of this house of God, it shall not be lawful to impose toll, tribute, or custom, upon them.

Ezra 8:21-23

Then I proclaimed a fast there, at the river of Ahava, that we might afflict ourselves before our God, to seek of him a right way for us, and for our little ones, and for all our substance. For I was ashamed to require of the king a band of soldiers and horsemen to help us against the enemy in the way: because we had spoken unto the king, saying, The hand of our God is upon all them for good that seek him; but his power and his wrath is against all them that forsake him. So we fasted and besought our God for this: and he was intreated of us.

I John 2:15-18

Love not the world, neither the things that are in the world. If any man love the world, the love of the Father is not in him. For all that is in the world, the lust of the flesh, and the lust of the eyes, and the pride of life, is not of the Father, but is of the world. And the world passeth away, and the lust thereof: but he that doeth the will of God abideth for ever. Little children, it is the last time: and as ye have heard that antichrist shall come, even now are there many antichrists; whereby we know that it is the last time.

I John 2:23-29

Whosoever denieth the Son, the same hath not the Father: he that acknowledgeth the Son hath the Father also. Let that therefore abide in you, which ye have heard from the beginning. If that which ye have heard from the beginning shall remain in you, ye also shall continue in the Son, and in the Father. And this is the promise that he hath promised us, even eternal life. These things have I written unto you concerning them that seduce you. But the anointing which ye have received of him abideth in you, and ye need not that any man teach you: but as the same anointing teacheth you of all things, and is truth, and is no lie, and even as it hath taught you, ye shall abide in him. And now, little children, abide in him; that, when he shall appear, we may have confidence, and not be ashamed before him at his coming. If ye know that he is righteous, ye know that every one that doeth righteousness is born of him.

I Peter 3:18-19

For Christ also hath once suffered for sins, the just for the unjust, that he might bring us to God, being put to death in the flesh, but quickened by the Spirit: By which also he went and preached unto the spirits in prison;

I Peter 2:6-10

Wherefore also it is contained in the scripture, Behold, I lay in Sion a chief corner stone, elect, precious: and he that believeth on him shall not be confounded. Unto you therefore which believe he is precious: but unto them which be disobedient, the stone which the builders disallowed, the same is made the head of the corner, And a stone of stumbling, and a rock of offence, even to them which stumble at the word, being disobedient: whereunto also they were appointed. But ye are a chosen generation, a royal priesthood, an holy nation, a peculiar people; that ye should shew forth the praises of him who hath called you out of darkness into his marvellous light: Which in time past were not a people, but are now the people of God: which had not obtained mercy, but now have obtained mercy.

Acts 13:48

And when the Gentiles heard this, they were glad, and glorified theword of the Lord: and as many as were ordained to eternal life believed.

www.ingramcontent.com/pod-product-compliance
Lightning Source LLC
LaVergne TN
LVHW041712060526
838201LV00043B/696